MEN OF COLOR IN HIGHER EDUCATION

MEN OF COLOR IN HIGHER EDUCATION

New Foundations for Developing Models for Success

EDITED BY

Ronald A. Williams

With LeManuel Lee Bitsói,
Edmund T. Gordon,
Shaun R. Harper,
Victor B. Sáenz, and
Robert T. Teranishi

Foreword by Freeman A. Hrabowski III

STERLING, VIRGINIA

Published by Stylus Publishing, LLC.
22883 Quicksilver Drive
Sterling, Virginia 20166-2102

Library of Congress Cataloging-in-Publication Data

Men of color in higher education: new foundations for developing
models for success / edited by Ronald A. Williams; foreword by
Freeman A. Hrabowski, III.
    pages cm
Includes bibliographical references and index.
ISBN 978-1-62036-159-7 (cloth: alk. paper)
ISBN 978-1-62036-160-3 (pbk.: alk. paper)
ISBN 978-1-62036-161-0 (library networkable e-edition)
ISBN 978-1-62036-162-7 (consumer e-edition)
1. African American men—Education (Higher) 2. African
American male college students. 3. Academic achievement—
United States. I. Williams, Ronald A., editor of compilation.
LC2781.M46 2014
378.1'982996073—dc23

                                                        2013038253

13-digit ISBN: 978-1-62036-159-7 (cloth)
13-digit ISBN: 978-1-62036-160-3 (paperback)
13-digit ISBN: 978-1-62036-161-0 (library networkable e-edition)
13-digit ISBN: 978-1-62036-162-7 (consumer e-edition)

Printed in the United States of America

All first editions printed on acid-free paper
that meets the American National Standards Institute
Z39-48 Standard.

First Edition, 2014

10   9   8   7   6   5   4   3   2   1

I would like to acknowledge the outstanding support of Gaston Caperton, retired president of the College Board, for his unstinting support of this project, and without whose vision and engagement it would not have been possible. Similarly, I want to thank the scholars whose intellect, energy, and engagement with the subject matter were an inspiration to behold. Each brought his or her own perspective but with such generosity of spirit that all the intellectual hurdles we encountered were resolved with the minimum of fuss and in total amity. Thanks also to Freeman Hrabowski, my colleague of many years, for agreeing to write the foreword on very short notice. That was much appreciated. Last, I'd like to say thank you to Marilyn Cushman, my longtime assistant, whose proofreading, arrangements for meetings and conference calls, budgetary supervision, and general encouragement made a complex project if not simple certainly manageable. This was a great team with which to work.

CONTENTS

FOREWORD

W hen I arrived at the University of Maryland, Baltimore County (UMBC), 25 years ago, I realized that large numbers of African American male students were not doing well academically, particularly in science, technology, engineering, and mathematics (STEM). With Baltimore philanthropist Robert Meyerhoff, who was interested in supporting young Black males, we started the Meyerhoff Scholars Program in 1988 to determine ways of increasing the number of African American males succeeding in these disciplines. Research showed then that many of these young Black men were not succeeding in high school, and that they were often seen as disruptive and less engaged than other groups. There was also evidence that disproportionately low numbers of these students enrolled in advanced courses, and too few were entering and succeeding in college. It is troubling that research today shows similar results. *Men of Color in Higher Education* adds substantially to our understanding of where we are today and demonstrates that significant work remains if we are to ensure that students of all backgrounds are able to succeed in higher education.

We must embrace that substantial—but not insurmountable—challenge. For more than 20 years, the Meyerhoff program, which was broadened early to include women, students from other minority groups, and majority students interested in diversity issues, has helped students to achieve at the highest levels. Of the 800 students who have graduated from the program, more than 80 percent have gone on to graduate programs, and large numbers have received STEM Ph.Ds. and M.D.-Ph.Ds. Most important, half of the African American students have been male. The approach we have taken with all the students has been strengths-based, because we are continually helping students understand the assets they bring to the campus, from resilience and a determination to succeed to being tough-skinned because of previous challenging situations. *Men of Color in Higher Education* argues for just such a strengths-based approach. This new book presents compelling, and also troubling, evidence that colleges and universities have for too long focused on deficits as they study the performance of men of color and develop programs to improve their achievement.

We can and must change that reality. From the beginning, our experience with the Meyerhoff program stimulated conversations among administrators, faculty, and staff about the ways the academic structures and processes needed to change to better support students of color. I remember a STEM faculty member years ago remarking that Black men sat at the back of the class and rarely asked questions or took notes. Rather than accept that as a given, we asked why. What barriers did students of color, particularly men, face in the classroom environment? What expectations were we setting for them? Did the professor, for example, interact with Black students regardless of where they chose to sit? Should students be expected to passively take notes, or should faculty be more actively engaging them?

Our experience with the Meyerhoff program taught us the importance of faculty–student engagement and of building community among students to help them succeed academically, particularly in STEM. Other key components of the program include (a) peer support; (b) involving caring adults; (c) assembling groups of students to talk freely about what they think and believe and how they see the environment; (d) empowering students to do well in school; (e) giving students incentives for high achievement; (f) family involvement; and (g) providing community service opportunities, especially mentoring or supporting young boys.

Men of Color in Higher Education embraces asset-based models like the one developed at UMBC, and it holds education professionals accountable for being precise about what we mean when we talk about improving student success and providing better support for students of color. Whether examining the outcomes of Asian and Pacific Islander or African American students, the contributors make a compelling case for nuance and precision. Not only must colleges and universities carefully examine student outcomes by gender and race, but they must go further in disaggregating data. Pacific Islander students, for example, have much weaker college-going rates and college outcomes than Asian American students of East or South Asian backgrounds. Likewise, African American students whose families have a long history in the United States fare quite differently in our education system than first- or second-generation African immigrants.

This book reminds us of the importance of historical, social, and familial contexts. We humans are profoundly shaped by our earliest experiences. My life was changed when, at 12 years old, I decided to participate in the Children's March in Birmingham, Alabama. I marched because I understood the power of education and wanted the best one possible. I also marched because, even as a boy, I believed that we in America could be better than we were. My decision resulted in my being jailed for five terrifying days, but the entire experience taught me that the world does not always have to be as it is today. We need to ensure that more children are empowered to dream of what is possible and to act.

At UMBC we've also learned important lessons about social, cultural, and family influence from interviews with mothers and fathers of African American males in the Meyerhoff program. Though the individual experiences of families varied, many reported that they had emphasized high academic expectations, overcoming adversity, setting strong limits and discipline, maintenance of family rituals, open and consistent and strong communications, and open discussion of values. Interestingly, we have also learned lessons from some of these parents who can talk about their experiences with other sons who have not been as successful academically. We can often learn more from challenging and difficult cases than we can from successful ones.

At UMBC, we've worked closely with hundreds of high-achieving minority college students in the Meyerhoff program, and simultaneously with a much younger group of at-risk students in the Choice Program, which we began in 1987 through UMBC's Shriver Center (named for Sargent and Eunice Kennedy Shriver). The program provides round-the-clock support for young boys (mostly center-city African American youth), empowering them and engaging their families through a variety of services. Youth who enter the program typically fall into two categories: Some are first-time offenders, and others come from households where drug use and other factors have put them at high risk. What we've learned from working with these boys over the past 20 years is similar to lessons learned in the Meyerhoff program and with other African American males on campus. Teachers and professors can provide the best support to students by gaining their trust; letting students know how much they care; setting high expectations for the students; continual emphasizing how much they believe in them; focusing on the importance of hard work and respect for authority; and, finally, helping them develop a sense of self and a vision for their future.

Importantly, we've learned that the approaches that have helped more men of color succeed also can help more women and students of all races and backgrounds succeed. That is, perhaps, the most powerful promise presented in *Men of Color in Higher Education*. If we can help our most vulnerable students succeed, we can ensure that all students experience the type of education that is at the heart of the American dream.

Freeman A. Hrabowski III
President
University of Maryland, Baltimore County

Ronald A. Williams

In 2007 a number of reports were published citing the many challenges faced by African American males. At the same time, the College Board was engaged in a series of discussions about how it could best respond to the challenges faced by a number of communities of color, and the theme of performance of men of color in higher education fit quite seamlessly into those conversation

With this in mind, the College Board embarked on a series of conversations in 2008, which came to be known as Dialogue Days, about the inadequate educational progress of males of color in the United States. Those sessions led to a well-received report that prompted a series of follow-up papers and seminars sponsored by the College Board. In the aftermath of these reports, however, what struck us was that while we had described the problem in a variety of ways, more work needed to be done if we were to advance the conversation in any significant way. What emerged from that sobering observation was a desire, indeed a demand, to create a project that would change the direction of the dialogue. One reason for this was that in the past 10 years or so since the conversation about the plight of young men had started, there seemed to be little advance in the conversation or any change in the conditions that were being lamented.

This observation gave rise to a series of questions. What were we doing wrong? Were we doing anything? Where did the fault lie? Why had all the activity produced no change in the discourse from that of a crisis to one of hopefulness? There were some examples of successful responses to this issue, but why were they always small and seemingly marginal? Why couldn't these small successes be replicated, since they were always cited and examined? Addressing these questions led to others. Was the mode of analysis all wrong? More specifically, were we dealing with a gender issue, or rather one of poverty? Did it make sense to identify this as a gender concern when females of color, while doing better than boys, were themselves at risk? Just as important, would we understate the challenge if we looked at only the two most politically visible groups, Latinos and African Americans, or could we learn something from examining other groups, for example, Native Americans and Asian Americans as well?

It was this series of questions that led to the conception of this book. Once we determined that these four groups were to be examined, we then selected the best scholars who were writing on these populations. That led us to LeManuel Bitsóí, Edmund Gordon, Shaun Harper, Victor Sáenz, and Robert Teranishi, who were quite ably assisted by Beth Bukoski, Celeste Henery, Lloyd Lee, and Loni Bordoloi Pazich. Each of the lead scholars had developed a reputation for solid work in the field, and while they approached the subject in a variety of ways, this turned out for the better because we wanted multiple perspectives on the issue. The process began with a series of conversations to identify the salient points of emphasis as well as the areas of overlap between and among the various scholars. Since they came from different disciplines, their languages and analytical frameworks were different as well, which is reflected in this volume. From the beginning, however, certain concerns emerged. If we were to understand the process of response to the challenges each had outlined in various writings before this project, then we had to determine what it meant to be male at the beginning of the 21st century. This surfaced as a critical issue since each scholar believed that this understanding, or indeed misapprehension, was at least in part the cause of what seemed to be males' disengagement from the classroom. It was felt that some understanding of the constructed reality of present-day maleness had to be determined. The conversations in which these scholars engaged were richly textured, exquisitely nuanced, and powerfully stimulating. While they covered lots of philosophical ground, after several meetings the group agreed there was no male archetype that was accepted in our society in the early 21st century. Until the 1970s conceptions of maleness were largely unexamined, although one might say that a folk understanding of maleness existed. With the coming of women's liberation theory and later feminist theory, however, this archetype was shattered. Queer theory has further redefined gender roles in the society. The male archetype, therefore, has been replaced only by uncertainty. No male theory has emerged, and as a result, we were faced with the question of what the analytical framework that would undergird its analysis should be. In this context, observing the male issue through the prism of feminist theory emerged, and this is what provides the structural analytical framework for the work.

The decision to use feminism as the underlying framework of the book, however, did not solve all the conceptual problems. We also faced the issue of how to treat the various groups we had identified for analysis. Would all four groups bear up under this framework? While each group could be identified, readers' knowledge of the groups could be assumed to be very different, so how would the book provide a platform for each reader so that he or she would be able to respond to the information in an informed way?

Our initial conversations suggested that all groups were not equally well known. While a body of research on African Americans and Latinos had begun to investigate their conditions, Native Americans and Asian Americans were less well researched and were, therefore, frequently left out of the policy conversations. It was felt that to understand fully the problem of males of color, we needed to investigate these groups as rigorously as we would the Latino and African American groups. We agreed on the need to describe the Asian American and Native American groups statistically since their stories were less familiar. One caveat was that the use of statistics had to avoid the usual deficit thinking reflected in the way these groups were most often portrayed. Statistical analysis would as well consciously avoid an explicit or implicit confrontation between males and females. This left unanswered the question of how to make our point about the existing disparities, and it was determined that we would include high-performing groups as normative to not distort the success of women of color. One result of these decisions is that the book applies the use of statistics differentially, with the African American and Latino populations described in more theoretical terms than the other two populations. As a result, this book seeks to provide more of a historical overview for the latter two groups than it does for the first two. This, it is hoped, will make the book more useful for its intended audience.

Chapter 1, "The Problem of Patriarchy," provides the underlying theoretical framework for the book by rethinking our ideas about the problems young men of color face. The authors, Gordon and Henery, use the "crisis" of young Black men to illustrate how patriarchy, in its intersection with racism, economic inequality, and heteronormative orientations, structures the circumstances of young men of color and the ways they are understood. They accomplish this by retheorizing patriarchy as not only processes of unequal gender relations but as forces shaping men's relationships with women and, uniquely, with other men. Through their analysis of patriarchy, they demonstrate how Black women are often elided in discussions of men's crises and how patriarchal norms are the source of Black men and other men of color's problems. The authors bring Black women centrally into the understanding of Black men's crises and highlight the issues they face. Finally, the chapter reveals how hierarchical competition and dominance between men and masculine *Respectability* structure men's lives, leading to many of the problems understood to be the basis of the crises of men of color.

Chapter 2, "Intersectionality," deals with another kind of invisibility faced by the Asian American community. Almost universally seen as successful because of the advances made by its four largest subgroups—Chinese, Japanese, Koreans, and Indians—Asian American issues are often left off the table when policy discussions occur. Like Native Americans, Asian

Americans are relatively unknown except in the stereotypical sense that they are the *model minority*, a moniker that covers up a number of disadvantages some members of the group face (e.g., social statistics of Pacific Islanders and Southeast Asians are frequently little different from those describing African Americans and Latinos). Yet these groups' issues are made invisible because, by all accounts, the "Asian" is successful. This chapter's authors, Teranishi and Pazich, seek to deconstruct this assumption, and for this reason, it is more heavily statistical than the others. One challenge they face is the lack of prior theorizing on why some groups are failing and others are succeeding in the United States. Teranishi and Pazich seek to construct a theoretical framework using intersectionality as the basis of analysis. To this end, they investigate differences within the Asian groups, showing how different modes of arrival have differential impacts on populations' educational success. They then hazard an explanation of why women are apparently adjusting better to these circumstances than men. Still, while they attempt to explain why men are performing less well than women, they laud women's success, recognizing that it is important for the whole group to be successful.

Chapter 3, "Ahistoricism in the Native American Experience," investigates the Native American condition. The Native Americans' history as the human presence in the Americas at the time of White conquest, whose purpose was political and cultural domination through wars between Europeans and American Indians, complicates the analysis of males of color. In this chapter, then, Bitsóí and Lee attempt to provide a short sketch of that conflict, identifying what was lost in the subsequent colonization. They investigate the roles of women and men in the precolonial period; the struggle that Native Americans faced to retain even rudimentary elements of their culture; and, most important for the purposes of this book, how those roles were changed in such a way that maleness, which was clearly defined before the conquest, subsequently became a source of great anxiety and uncertainty. They also discuss how Native Americans are attempting to reconstruct that cultural strength through Native American institutions and practices.

Chapter 4, "Masculinity: Through a Latino Male Lens," returns to the theme of challenging existing notions of masculinity advanced in Chapter 1, but here it is seen through the particular lens of the Latino male experience. Sáenz and Bukoski examine the feminist movement and present, as a counterpoint, the male response in the 1970s and 1980s. They argue that current ideas of masculinity—as expressed through the strong silent type, machismo, and *familismo* attributes operating under pressure to succeed in a world that is stingy with its opportunities for young men of color—create an almost pathological desire either to be hypercompetitive or to drop out. As in Chapter 1, Sáenz and Bukoski suggest that this hypercompetitiveness often takes antisocial pathways, since American society does not provide the opportunities, nor do these young men have the social capital, to compete in conventional ways. This lack of social capital makes young males of color excessively prideful and creates the need for them to be hyperindependent, which has deleterious effects because these young men are often not able to admit to needing help, and in a learning situation, this can prove disastrous. Finally, they examine the behavior of a group of Latino males through this lens, particularly showing the close linkages between their pride and their social fear.

Chapter 5, "(Re)Setting the Agenda for College Men of Color: Lessons Learned from a 15-Year Movement to Improve Black Male Student Success," attempts to address many of the questions raised by the scholars' conversations, although its primary mode of attack is to investigate the many conferences, papers, and so forth on this issue to determine what has been said and also to give us a sense of what has or has not been done as a result. Harper places particular emphasis on investigating the current use of deficits to define the experience of males of color. He argues that this is a fundamentally flawed approach that can only lead to despair. Therefore, in this chapter, he seeks to identify the assets these young men have and use them to create models of response. He also proposes that the current literature and the programs are largely atheoretical ad hoc responses based on instinct, which, while designed with the best intentions, are often incapable of addressing the challenges many of these students bring to the classroom. Harper particularly argues that by ignoring the intersectionality of the challenges facing these students, the programs are often deficient.

Finally, we faced the issue of who should or, indeed, would read this book. One of the challenges with attempting a reconceptualization of the ideas inherent in the current analysis of the problem was that it ran the risk of being too heavily theoretical, thereby alienating many professionals who would be interested in programmatic responses, not simply conceptual analysis. Another issue was combining the groups in a single book. Instead of a chapter on each group, which would allow a reader to easily focus on the chapter about a certain group and ignore the theories about the other groups that could prove helpful in the analysis of his or her group, we wanted policy analysts as well as professionals to find value in this book while simultaneously changing the discourse about the population we were investigating. A number of audiences, therefore, ought to find value in this work. People who are working with specific populations should see in it some relevance to the work they are doing, and it ought to provide signposts for them as they try to create programs in response to their group's issues. Researchers should be able to glean from the book a set of new directions for analysis of the males of color issue, and policymakers will see new ways of thinking about how policy and funding mechanisms ought to be reconsidered to be more effective in responding to this issue. In other words, the book is designed to carry a lot of freight. Still, given the seriousness of the concerns facing those interested in the fate of men of color, it is not unreasonable to expect, and indeed to demand, this degree of seriousness.

THE PROBLEM OF
PATRIARCHY

Edmund T. Gordon and Celeste Henery

For over half a century, a state of crisis has defined young Black men's lives. Their high rates of incarceration, unemployment, and undereducation have drawn the attention of academics as well as professionals and policymakers. More recently, similar concerns about other young men of color have emerged. While theories, methodologies, and agendas have been developed to improve the conditions of these populations, the interventions based upon them have yet to substantially shift outcomes. The central premise of this chapter is that the nature of the problems facing Black men and other young men of color has yet to be fully understood. To this end, we offer a conceptual framework to reconsider the circumstances facing these young men.

This chapter interrogates the structures of power in the United States that position young Black men and other men of color as being in crisis. Race-based power inequity and its operations through gender and sexuality provide some of the key framing processes that along with economic subordination (poverty and economic insecurity) shape the choices and behaviors of young men of color. They also affect how the dominant society reads these men. This understanding of the structural conditions of crisis, specifically of young Black men, is relatively well established in the literature (Ferguson, 2001; Lewis, 2003; Noguera, 2008; Rios, 2011). We contribute to this analysis a reconceptualization of patriarchy as a critical, overlooked axis of differentiation and unequal gendered power influencing young men of color's practices, experiences, and social positioning. As scholars of Black life, we focus on the example of young Black men but create an analytical framework that addresses the structural factors shaping the lives of young men of color more generally. Understanding the crises of young men of color, we suggest, hinges on an analysis of how gendered power relations intersects with racism and economic inequality to socially position these men in competitive relationships of dominance and subordination to women as well as to other men. Patriarchy underpins both these sets of relationships and the social fields where they are enacted. It constructs the normative forms of masculine practice that enable social and material upward mobility through the accumulation of social, cultural, and economic capital. An examination of patriarchy also allows us to reconsider the widespread understanding of men's crises by examining specifically how young Black men become visible and in need of surveillance, while Black women's issues are deemphasized. Within this framework we begin to unravel how young Black men are paradoxically both at risk and risky, and how their example informs the conditions of young men of color in general.

Patriarchy and Male Gender Roles

Gendered roles and expectations are pivotal to the differential social positioning, experience, and identity formation of people of color. Unfortunately, much of the avalanche of literature, media attention, and programming focused on the problems of young men of color assumes that these men, without considering the issue of gendered power at all, are somehow experiencing more difficulty and greater challenges than women of color. By contrast, intersectional feminist theory unveils how power operates through gender, sharpening our critical gaze on how economically poor women of color live at the crossroads of multiple forms of oppression (patriarchy, racism, classism, gender roles, heterosexism, homophobia, etc.). The broad (White) men's movement of the 1970s and 1980s unveiled some questions about gender focusing on sexism and male chauvinism. However, it is only recently, through the expansion of feminist, queer, and transgender scholarship and activism, that the critical study of gender is gaining traction. This work has broadened the field of inquiry on gender into the structures that create heteronormative gender roles and values that produce differing forms of gender privilege, hierarchy, and oppression. These theorists have located and interpreted the differential webs of power that construct contemporary conceptions of gender and gender norms in ill-fitting and often oppressive ways (Butler, 1993, 2004; Fausto-Sterling, 2000; Feinberg, 2003; Halberstam, 1998). One of the critical interventions from this body of scholarship is a deepening conversation on the construction and experience of masculinities and masculine practice.

Building on this foundation, this chapter explores gender-based power inequity by reinvigorating the concept of *patriarchy*, but does so atypically, to examine how it constrains the lives of men. We use this uncharacteristic approach to investigate the circumstances facing young men of color as well as to understand why those circumstances facing women of color and men of color are socially understood and considered differently. This theoretical emphasis is counterintuitive particularly when applying the conventional definition of *patriarchy* as the "rule of the father" or men's domination of women and children. It is also complicated given that men have been rightfully viewed to be beneficiaries rather than so-called victims of patriarchy. However, this traditional conceptualization limits analyses of patriarchy's influence on the social relations between and among men as well as male cultural practices, which play out across a variety of complicated fields like race, economic status, and sexuality. By expanding our lens beyond men's normative relationships with their families and specifically women, we explore how patriarchal thinking and values—dominance, control, hierarchical competition, and subservience—configure gender roles and social expectations, giving particular attention to how patriarchy construes men's relationships with themselves and each other. Through this approach, we retheorize patriarchy as a technique of power and a form of mastery rooted in what bell hooks (2004) calls "White supremacist, capitalist patriarchy" (p. 17).

This chapter is organized into several sections. The first section dives a bit deeper into how patriarchy has been historically constructed, considering how it is often not named but is operative in analyses about young men of color. Next, we expound on our reinterpretation of patriarchy to discuss what we characterize as patriarchal masculinity: the dominant norm cueing male gender orientation and performance. We suggest that patriarchal masculinity is the operative form of masculinity asserted and undergirding the crisis of young men of color. This narrative uncovers the problems of young men of color as a part of patriarchal ethos.

Then we turn to patriarchy's influence in the development and creation of statistics. This framing helps to contextualize how men become statistically relevant differently from women. From this foundation, the differences between how Black women and Black men are positioned by patriarchy and its values become clearer. It also demonstrates how patriarchy plays out in men's relationships with themselves and other men.

The chapter's final sections home in on *Respectability* as a cultural form of patriarchy that shapes Black men's identities, roles, and relationships with each other.[1] We conclude by calling for an intensified exploration of patriarchy's impact on social relations, particularly on men, and its implications on their educational experiences. We work to keep women present throughout our entire analysis to remind us how patriarchy continues to socially disadvantage women, as they are not its principal beneficiaries, and also to reframe the crisis as one that is shared.

Redefining *Patriarchy*

Our conceptual framework highlights patriarchy as part of an interlocking system of oppression conditioning the social world of young men of color in the United States. Patriarchy is the underevaluated and less recognized structuring variable interconnected to racism and economic subjugation (predatory capitalism); together, these forces create the social matrix with which young men of color are interfacing and that we are investigating as the field of the problem. Patriarchy's coevolution with racial capitalism produced an articulated system of thought and social structure that directly and indirectly influences and generates men's and women's socialization and the very logics and ethos of the institutions and cultural milieu of this nation. The connections between racism and capitalism and their debatable separateness are widely written about (Robinson, 2000; Williams, 1944/1994). However, patriarchy, gestured at through notions of paternalism and mastery (Hartman, 1997; Jackman, 1994), has had limited comprehensive analysis within the historical and social interface of racial slavery, colonization, apartheid, and democratization in the United States. The United States' social foundations in racial slavery, its framing economic and social system of racial capitalism, and its expansion into privatization and free trade have created a cultural and social environment in which power articulates around racial gender roles and their function in a materially hierarchical capitalist economy. In other words, the social expectations for how people are to show up in society in gendered ways is also part of a cultural ethos that continues to privilege male bodies and a set of values associated with what is constructed as masculine. While we encourage deeper historical work into these distinct origins of patriarchy and how they have shaped men's relationships, our focus here is to frame a contemporary conceptualization of patriarchy that enables us to think through how young men of color are shaped by these forces and how they react and respond to them. We understand these forces as hegemonic at the same time that we envision these young men of color as agents.

With this in mind, we aim to construct a critical theoretical field for a more expansive theorization of patriarchy in service to the understanding of contemporary predicaments of men and women of color. The traditional and principal definition of *patriarchy* is a social system whose structures and institutions, such as the family or state, are led by or dominated by men. This dominance and control include economic, social, cultural, and political institutions, such as business, government, the judiciary and the law, religious institutions, the family, and others. Patriarchy constructs the commonsensical connection between the male self, the father, the family, and the nation. It defines and naturalizes essentialized gender roles of women and men, and construes women largely in relationship, specifically in opposition, to men. Within this structure in the United States, sexist and homophobic politics and beliefs about women as well as men who enact nonnormative masculinity have flourished. Furthermore, the varying degrees of chauvinist thinking also actively devalue and disempower those attributes associated with, and those qualities culturally and socially ascribed to, women, namely the feminine.[2] These sexist patriarchal practices have kept and continue to keep men in leadership roles and decision-making positions as well as frequently invest in sustaining men's economic and social options and power. Additionally, the homophobic, racial, and classed qualities of these practices in the United States simultaneously work to hierarchize and empower only certain male bodies.

The attack on and deconstruction of traditional patriarchal values in regard to women was the battle cry of feminism and branches of the women's movements of the 1960s and 1970s. The overwhelmingly White middle-class heterosexual women's second-wave feminist movement centered patriarchy as a system of power supporting male social control, including that of women's bodies and lives. Patriarchy structured women's exclusion in the workforce, underpayment, and social positioning in the home. It legitimated paternalistic, sexist, and limiting, if not repressive, gendered social roles for women on the basis of sex. What became the political and social argument emergent from this articulation of patriarchy was that women were the victims of this system enacted by men.

While the women's movement did much to topple traditional patriarchy, it should be noted there has been significant resistance. Some of the patriarchal backlash to feminism has been its misguided association with man hating and conflation with the advancement of matriarchies or female dominance. One of the overarching effects pertinent to our contribution is that the analysis of patriarchy has also almost entirely revolved around its effects on *women*. This distortion of patriarchy has crosscut race and ethnicity and has shut out a wider theoretical framing of its social implications in the lives of men and women and its relevance to the discussion of crisis.

Nonetheless, Black feminists have offered critical analytical tools for rethinking patriarchy in the lives of men. Observing how mainstream feminist foci on patriarchy often omitted racism, Black feminists became some of the first social actors and scholars to pay attention to, and to theorize patriarchy's coarticulation with, other structures of power (i.e., racism and capitalism) or, put another way, to realize how race is a gendered experience. Focusing on how patriarchal power intersected with White supremacy and racial privilege, they articulated and politicized how varied forces of oppression shaped their reality, including male domination and control within Black movements. bell hooks (1990) calls attention to the ways patriarchy played out in the gendering of the antiracist political objectives in Black movements, writing, "The discourse of Black resistance has almost always equated freedom with manhood" and is continued by Black and White men through the "patriarchal belief that revolutionary struggle was really about . . . the ability of men to establish political dominance" (p. 58). Failing to create a movement that addressed how Black men *and* women experienced racism differently that worked toward racial *and* gender equity or one that challenged hierarchical distributions of power and privilege, these Black movements inadequately addressed patriarchy and Black women's racial gendered experiences of social subjugation. Founding their own agendas and movement in the 1970s, Black women mobilized to decode the *intersection* of structures that systematically and oppressively scripted their lives.

Black feminists' highly disseminated and integrated theory of intersectionality (Combahee River Collective, 1977; Crenshaw, 1991) provides a critical lens and method for framing how oppression operates and is lived:

> The most general statement of our politics at the present time would be that we are actively committed to struggling against racial, sexual, heterosexual, and class oppression, and see as our particular task the development of integrated analysis and practice based upon the fact that the major systems of oppression are interlocking. The synthesis of these oppressions creates the conditions of our lives. As Black women we see Black feminism as the logical political movement to combat the manifold and simultaneous oppressions that all women of color face. (Combahee River Collective, 1977)

In highlighting how gender and its politics cannot be separated from their experiences of race or their racial politics, they midwifed the theory of intersectionality, focusing on the experiences and conditions of Black women. Black feminists' theory of intersectionality helped to uncover how race and patriarchal thinking structure gender roles and experiences of Black women in multiple ways. We use it as a rich theoretical platform to explore patriarchy's influence and articulation in the lives of men of color.

Patriarchal Masculinity

Previous College Board reports on males of color offer an insightful jumping-off point to give texture to our conceptualization of patriarchy's influence on young men of color. The assertions and language reported boldly capture the values and orientations being theorized here as patriarchal. Expectations to act "cool," "macho," and to be "the big man" characterize particular stances of performing masculinity, as do the encouragements to have "toughness" and "disrespect for women," and participate in illegal activity (College Board, 2010, p. 11). Machismo and *familismo* were specific values encouraged of Latino men, while the figure of the warrior continues as a masculine standard Native American men are to fulfill. In the case of Asian American and Pacific Islander young men, the reports cite theories of these groups as "lack[ing] the qualities associated with the form of masculinity most valued in U.S. society" (College Board, 2010, p. 15). This observation is one of the most direct references to the unnamed qualities or values of patriarchy and its conditioning of masculinity in the United States. The problemization of Asian Americans' and Pacific Islanders' masculinity captures how men of color, because of different racial gender constructs, are positioned in relation to the norm of what is conceived to be a valid masculinity—one that we are naming as patriarchal in construct and values.[3] To summarize, drawing on the words of bell hooks (2004), "the crisis facing men is not the crisis of masculinity, it is the crisis of patriarchal masculinity" (p. 32).

Following hooks, patriarchal masculinity is the dominant cultural and social conceptualization of masculinity in the United States that we are problemizing. While *men* and *male* are used to refer to a biological notion of bodies, what it means to be a man, or to adequately perform manhood in socially recognizable and valuable ways, is deeply embedded in long-standing cultural and social norms and practices in the United States. The conflation of male behavior with an essentialized notion of masculinity has been naturalized to such an extent that it has taken a significant amount of scholarship to awaken to the idea that "when something is about masculinity it is not always 'about men'" (Sedgwick, 1995, p. 12). Indeed, masculinity is not the possession of men, and it is neither uniform nor democratic in its social construction. Patriarchy, in many ways, is the force that has claimed masculinity as the sole property of the male body and how it should be expressed and lived (Halberstam, 1998; Pascoe, 2007). More than operating as what some scholars have defined as *hegemonic masculinity* (Connell & Messerschmidt, 2005), although it is that too, patriarchal masculinity encompasses a set of White heterosexual capitalist values, orientations, and expectations that men negotiate. Our interest lies with some of the central patriarchal values that drive men of color's socialization, interaction, and character with regard to women, families, the workplace, the streets, and, of particular divergent concern, with themselves and other men.

What is stated in the College Board (2010) report *The Educational Crisis Facing Young Men of Color* as the "search for respect" (p. 11) and the broader ways in which men are showing up in society as "outperform[ed]" (p. 2) and "lag[ging] behind" (p. 17) captures some of the effects of the values of competition, hierarchy, and Respectability central to the creation of patriarchal masculine roles, expectations, and practices. The conversations circulating around boys' and men's relationships, mentoring, fathering, and, of course, the meanings of boys becoming men, evoke the web of patriarchal mores. So when one participant caringly shares the need for these young men to "rediscover who they are as men" (College Board, 2010, p. 12) our response is to incite a conversation on what roles and expectations, what motivations and aspirations, are evoked and desired within this process of rediscovery. By understanding the cultural and social forces at work, the rediscovery can expand the field of possibilities for men's sense of self, their social presence and expression, and their greater contribution to society.

While we focus on the patriarchal construction of heterogender roles regarding men and women, we are attuned to the ways patriarchy has essentialized a heterodualistic construction of sex and gender (male/female) and an oppositional relationship between the two—the proverbial war of the sexes. Moreover, we recognize the presence of people who do not identify with or experience the specific sex categories of male or female. Patriarchy's production of a limited scope for gender identities, expressions, and roles is part and parcel of how it constrains men at the same time it instills them with privilege. Beginning to map and reveal the ramifications of patriarchy in the lives of men of color, in addition to those of women, and how it shapes social relations and meanings carries the prospect of simultaneously working toward the agenda of improving the lives of men of color as well as society in general.

Patriarchy and the Narrative of Crisis

We now turn to the relationship between patriarchy and the production of *the narrative of crisis*. The broader scholarly concern about urban Black men's conditions dates from the mid-20th century (Brown, 2011; Brown & Donnor, 2011; Gordon, Gordon, & Nembhard, 1994).[4] The academic inquiry, specifically of Black scholars (Drake & Cayton, 1970; Du Bois, 1899/1995; Frazier, 1997; Johnson, 1967), into the economic and educational disparities of the urban Black community was expanded through the Great Migrations of the

20th century. This inquiry was later transformed into a public discourse on the pathology of Black culture following the publication of D. P. Moynihan's (1965) *The Negro Family: The Case for National Action*. The Moynihan report, as it came to be known, was commissioned by the Johnson administration in an attempt to explain the continued struggles of Black people in spite of landmark legislation such as the Civil Rights Act, Aid to Families with Dependent Children, and other programs that were thought to be creating racial and economic equal opportunity in the United States. Naming unemployment, educational underperformance, and criminality among a host of other behaviors and family relations interpreted as socially aberrant, the Moynihan report fueled a discourse of crisis and blame regarding the social status of Black men, which in turn became the crisis of the Black community at large and subsequently that of the United States. Through the use and interpretation of data, much of which was statistics, the Moynihan report, as a document designed for federal public policy, popularized a particular framework—cultural deficit, cultural poverty, cultural pathology—for understanding the problems and solutions of the circumstances of Black men and the Black community. The expansion of this form of deficit thinking, in which the problems of communities of color are understood to be the result of their cultural and moral deficits rather than structural issues related to racism and poverty, has become hegemonic, so much so that much of the scholarship on these problems and the programs to address them are guided by the perceived deficiencies of the communities themselves. Moynihan's statistical analysis of the dire conditions of Black men, now commonly referred to as the Black male *crisis* or Black male *endangerment*, transformed into a discourse and a reality. Moynihan's cultural pathology paradigm became the hegemonic explanation of the plight of the Black community and the narrative behind the national call for law and order in the aftermath of the civil rights movement, the emergence of Black power, and urban race riots starting in the mid- to late 1960s. This "moral panic," manufactured by the Republican Party and others, and Moynihan's interpretation of its roots, became the basis for that party's policies of benign neglect with regard to the Black urban poor and ultimately for its political Southern strategy, both initiated under the Nixon administration. In this panic, pathologized Black communities in the form of such racial, gendered stereotypes as dependent welfare queens and violent and criminal Black bucks were understood to be a danger to the moral as well as the physical and material well-being of the White community and nation.

Since its dissemination, the Moynihan (1965) report has been widely critiqued for its pathological interpretation of lower-income Black culture and, in particular, its patriarchal and sexist demonization of Black women; however, it has yet to be analyzed for its patriarchal vision's impact on men. Its patriarchal focus has gone unquestioned as its framework continues in the representative narrative of crisis. Our contention is that the narrative conceals the tools that might address the actual problems. Thus, by understanding how patriarchy operates through the conditions it professes to describe, a new lens of study and inquiry emerges to examine the conditions of young men of color.

Suggesting a disabled Black manhood as the problem to be redressed, the Moynihan (1965) report problemized Black female-headed households and what were believed to be troubled gender roles. Principally, it advocated the reestablishment of Black men in patriarchal roles as the needed solution. The report centers on Black women and what is believed to be a "matriarchal structure . . . out of line with American society" as hindrances to Black men's ability to embody patriarchal manhood.

Since publication of the report, Black women and other scholars have attacked its flagrant pathological assertions and remedies, particularly concerning its patriarchal condemnation of economically poor Black women as the source of the problem (Alexander-Floyd, 2007; Collins, 2000; Radford-Hill, 2000). They also have called attention to how the ideological assumptions of much of Black politics have affirmed the same patriarchal values asserted in the report. What Black women argued was that Black men's investment in patriarchy, captured in ideas of claiming their proper manhood, would fail to comprehensively challenge dominant systems of political and social control sponsored by the intricate relationship between racist and capitalist foundations. Patriarchy, racism, and nationalist politics were mutually foundational and sustaining. Thus, without a much deeper critique of hierarchical gender relations and roles within the larger political frameworks that Black men were mobilizing as racial politics and political platforms, the type of social advancement Black men sought would remain unrealized. The absence of voices contesting the patriarchal objectives set forth in the Moynihan (1965) report, and the prototyping of the report for analyses of Black male crisis, explain the lack of critiques of patriarchy in the lives of men as well as the unquestioned investment in its paradigms.

Willie Legette's (1999) analysis of Black male patriarchy is an exception to this scholarly vacancy. Boldly, he names patriarchy within the narrative of crisis's operations and guides our unraveling of patriarchy as a social force. Legette critiques this narrative as a political discourse that centers the needs of the Black community on Black men and Black male life. His statement on the narrative is worth quoting at length:

> I conceptualize this ideology as Black manhood ideology, which refers not only to the crisis-of-the-Black-male thesis, but also to the broader context of Black politics and public discourse that rest on patriarchal assumptions.

> It refers to the emerging consensus that social and economic problems in the Black community are the result of Black men not being able to perform the roles expected of men in a patriarchal society. (p. 291)

According to Legette's deconstruction of the narrative of crisis and its interworkings, patriarchy is its structuring force, specifically through its construction of manhood and the roles men are socially expected to perform. He links the prevalence of the crisis narrative during the 1980s to the emergence of Black feminism and characterizes the narrative as antifeminist in sentiment and political thrust.

Critiquing the narrative as embroiled in Black male sexism, he lays out the overwhelming attention, resources, and energy galvanized around the crisis by institutions ranging from universities to foundations to churches. Legette's (1999) novel naming of patriarchy's sculpting and agency in the narrative provides an intellectual spark for expanding the conceptualization of patriarchy and its operations in society.

Deconstructing the Narrative of Crisis: Patriarchy and the Development of Statistics

Our exploration of the problems facing young men of color begins with how patriarchy not only shapes the discursive content of this notion of male crisis but also the wider context in which men's bodies are given meaning and are read. The crisis state of young men of color largely makes its case from the vast body of statistical evidence that is interpreted as representing these young men's uniquely challenging circumstances. A brief exploration of statistics allows us to understand why particular dimensions of the social conditions of Black men are legible to the state and hence publicly recognized as a crisis in ways that those of Black women typically are not.

The patriarchal formation and operations of the domain of public life, now conceptualized as the public sphere (Habermas, 1991), provide historical precedent to the foregrounding of the statistics of men, and Black men in particular. The public sphere constellates public life and civic engagement, which include activities such as voting, debate, representation, and organizing; it also acts as a mechanism by which the state governs. This framing of the public sphere has made it distinct from the private sphere of citizens' lives, frequently understood as the realm of the home. The birth of the public sphere in the United States, like many Western nations, occurred in the context of a patriarchal social framework (Pateman, 1988) that empowered and entrusted men with the control and orientation of civic life. As the public sphere's principal actors, men achieve governance through practices of domination and hierarchical competition with other men. Feminists have readily critiqued the gendered, racial, and classed assumptions and hierarchies structuring the public sphere (Benhabib, 1992, 1993; Fraser, 1990). They have paid particular attention to the patriarchal gendered division of labor in the United States that historically has reinforced a dichotomy between women's positions in the private domain and White property-owning men's authority in the public sphere. In addition, as a racial nation, the United States' de jure and de facto apartheid body politic excluded non-White men and women from this public sphere of activity, influence, and institutional power. Together, these origins founded a postbellum public sphere in the United States in which control continued to be mediated by racial, gendered, and economic hierarchies. The legal incorporation of men of color, and the social and economic diversification of the public sphere, only reified its male orientation and, consequently, competition among men. Social dynamics and negotiations for power played out through dominance over racially and economically subaltern men. This historical awareness enlightens the projected liberal perspective of an egalitarian field of citizen subjects and their expression by establishing the public sphere's construction and investment in patriarchy and its interrelation with capitalist and racial hierarchies. These foundations also begin to explicate how the public sphere has been oriented around and controlled by men's bodies and male culture. They inform how statistics, as the system of quantification of the public sphere, foreground men and male comparison and interaction differently from similar comparisons and interactions among women.

Statistics are one of the predominant interpretative mechanisms of Western governance and tend to reflect its vantages and interests. Developed in the 18th century, statistics represented an administrative and scientific field now characterized as the science of the state. Socially conceived of as a moral science, a truth in numbers, or, as Sir William Petty (1888) called it, "political arithmetic," statistics encompass systems of measurement designed to capture, categorize, and represent major social phenomena and concepts of and in a society. As Ian Hacking (1991) assesses, "The collection of statistics has created, at the least, a great bureaucratic machinery. It may think of itself as providing only information, but it is itself part of the technology of power in a modern state" (p. 181). The development of statistics across present-day Europe was part of a process of the consolidation of power and nation building facilitated through the assessment and quantification of populations (Desrosières, 1998; Porter, 1986). This tool was applied in different ways across nation–states but generally was framed in relation to the shifting scientific philosophical vantages from social determinism to systems inflected with chance and free will. Statistics accompanied the changing vision of what drives human behavior, developing population metrics informed by factors such as probability, chance, and risk. These measurements of human activity generated knowledge by numbers (statistics), which enabled agencies, governments, corporations, and so on to administer and control society. In other words, the particular patterns and conditions shown through numbers could be rendered predictable and managed through the interpretation of probabilities and chance made knowable by the numbers.

Statistics' emergence and use to quantify this public sphere speaks about the bodies and ideas that were being inquired into, analyzed, and named. Tukufu Zuberi (2001) details how racial ideology and projects have been central to the production and use of statistics from their origins in Europe and notions of eugenics to their current function in considering populations in the Americas and Africa. In the United States, for example, statistics were institutionalized as a tool of representation of the nation's citizenry in the Constitution with regard to voting and apportionment. Race and its intersection in the capitalist economic system played crosscutting roles in the construction and quantification of life in the public sphere, beginning in the context of slavery in the United States. Early negotiations on representation and the population included debates about the enslaved population and how its members were to be counted, given the geographic racial distribution of people in the United States, the population's relevance for taxation, and the economics of the developing nation (Anderson, 1988, pp. 12–13). It should be noted that even as extreme anti-Black racism permeated U.S. thinking during Reconstruction, patriarchal impulses enabled Black men to gain the legal right to vote and enter the public sphere long before women. This transformation signaled the patriarchal exclusion of women from the public sphere and the contingent, if not antagonistic, entry of Black and other men of color. Male competition and domination only heightened with the presence and agency of men of color, notably Black men, in the public domain.

The mandating of the census in the U.S. Constitution for the purposes of quantifying the population increased in importance following the nation's transition from the Civil War into the 20th century (Anderson, 1988, pp. 66–73). The economic fallout of the Great Depression and widespread unemployment raised questions about how accurately the data government used reflected the conditions of the population.[5] This misalignment fueled the need for the production of systems and information to better assess and *predict* as a means of managing risk. Statistics grew as a technology of quantification as well as a predictive instrument investigating the population and now are frequently used to give meaning to lived characteristics, such as health; intelligence; accomplishment; success; and our point of interest, risk.

Statistics today frequently act as negative predictors and calculators of things feared, such as unemployment, death, violence, and disease. In addition, statistics have become the central paradigm through which lives are assessed, predicted, and understood within the control and maintenance of the public sphere. Because of their social prevalence and saturation as well as their use as negative predictors, Kathleen Woodward (2009) contends that they create a sense of unsafety and "omnipresent risk" that she characterizes as "statistical hegemony" and "statistical panic" (p. 14). Similar to statistics that quantify the lives of young men of color as simultaneously at risk and risky, the deployment of statistics in the United States captures a population or phenomena that trouble, if not threaten, the status quo of the public sphere. Statistics quantify bodies to different degrees, and in differing terms, to support normative views of life. Men who are unmoored from traditional patriarchal values or unable through their differences to adequately perform racial, economic, and physical patriarchal norms draw such attention. Consequently, statistics on men of color and their importance emerge from this patriarchal and racial orientation of power in the public sphere, and their exploration begins to unravel how the lives of young men and women of color are quantified and differently understood.

In sum, rather than challenging statistics—in fact, they are an effective and necessary language for addressing our collective reality—our inquiry into their sociocultural formation gives insight into how the lives of young men and women of color are differently quantified, made legible, and understood in the United States in ways that the narrative of crisis collapses. Patriarchy, we contend, is a key overlooked conceptual force that has conditioned the formation of the public sphere and its statistical representation.

Gender and the Production of Statistics

Highlighting the differences between the contemporary statistics produced about Black women and those of Black men begins to unearth the patriarchal imprint and tendencies of the public sphere. The Moynihan (1965) report codified the juxtaposition of Black men and women and established a template for how and when Black women's statistics are produced and how they are used to interpret the larger social field. Black women's quantification and cultural pathologization as welfare recipients and single mothers have now expanded into contemporary constructions of Black women as also perpetually unmarried, unhealthy, and incarcerated. A simple contemporary search on Black women in *The New York Times* brings up articles on Black women and marriage, Black women and HIV, in addition to Black women's strides in education and business, which are all similar points of comparison (with the exception of HIV) in the Moynihan report. The statistics and public conversations about Black women parallel the narrative of crisis of Black men but do so by framing Black women in a competitive dynamic with Black men. We consider this framing of Black women and men to be a legacy of the patriarchal orientation of the public sphere and how statistics reflect this domain's considerations and preoccupations.

The marital status of Black women has been a consistent statistical concern over the past couple of years in the media and one that captures the patriarchal hyperattention to the gender roles of families and in particular the Moynihanian concentration on the believed dysfunctionality of the Black family. Popularly conceived of as the most unwed group, Black women, their singleness, and marriageability are topics of academic inquiry as well (Banks, 2011; Clarke, 2011). Stanford Law School professor Ralph Richard Banks's book *Is Marriage for White People?* gained national attention for its analysis and call, among other considerations, for Black women to date *outside the race* as a means of addressing their unpartnered status. More than the particularities of the findings, the sustained focus and concern with Black women's roles in creating families, their investment in the contract of marriage, their social advancement, and how these come to bear on their relationships with and to Black men intones many of the patriarchal concerns first carved out around the family structure and, by proxy, the nation. This focus reflects the portrayal of abnormal gender roles shown in the Moynihan (1965) report and supported by U.S. societal norms at large. The widely circulated statistics that Black women are "twice as likely as White women to never have married by age 45 and twice as likely to be divorced, widowed, or separated" (Nitsche & Brueckner, 2009, p. 2) illustrate a trend of public concentration on, if not highlighting of, Black women's relationship to the conventional family structure. The problemization of Black women's marital status connects to the traditional heteronormative patriarchal control of reproduction, couched in the male/female partnership and nuclear family. It evokes a patriarchal disciplining of nonnormative female behavior and, by extension, of men's practices in failing to maintain the patriarchal role in society. These preoccupations tell little about whether Black women experience their marital status as their most pressing issue.

Since the Moynihan (1965) report, this comparative emphasis on Black women's and men's conditions suggests how and when the statistics on Black women are produced. As mentioned, Black women's economic and educational improvements are pivotal to this comparison and also work against, and minimize, the varied struggles men and women face. Popular representations of professionally successful Black women, such as Oprah Winfrey or now the frequently cited Michelle Obama (Harris-Perry, 2011), distort the economic reality of Black women whose unemployment rates in 2012 remain high at 12.1 percent compared to 6.3 percent for White women (UC Berkeley Labor Center, 2013). By comparison, adult Black men's unemployment rates in 2012 were only slightly higher than adult Black women's, at 13.7 percent (UC Berkeley Labor Center, 2013). Citing these statistics shows a trend (rather than simply making a statistical point) in how Black women and their lives are represented in numbers and U.S. society. Affluent and privileged women, such as Winfrey and Obama, are exceptions that fail to capture the reality that in 2010, 25.6 percent of all Black women lived in poverty (National Women's Law Center, 2011, p. 2). This average percentage of Black women in poverty is second to that of Native American women, at 26.4 percent (National Women's Law Center, 2011, p. 3). Both of these percentages are comparatively high when viewed alongside the 10.4 percent of non-Hispanic White women living in poverty (National Women's Law Center, 2011, p. 3).

Legette's (1999) analysis strategically intervenes in the reading of statistics of Black women to challenge the premise that Black men are worse off and that they are the sole group in dire social straights. In fact, the analytical framing of Black women and men inaccurately places the two groups in competition, and all too often, following the Moynihan (1965) report, has Black women linked to, if not accountable for, the problems facing Black men. Moreover, Black men are often constructed as victims, whereas Black women, whether "successful" or "dependent on the state," are more often framed as agents in their own circumstances. By juxtaposing how Black men and women are often pitted against each other in a social and statistical war, evoking a zero-sum game, Legette suggests that Black women's conditions may be as dire as those of Black men.

Indeed, the lack of narratives about the endangerment of Black women is not evidence that Black women's social states, whether in health, economics, or incarceration, are not exigent. By contrast, Black women's plights often tell an interconnected story of Black men and women. However, the statistics on women rarely gain the same type of attention because men have been the principal agents and subjects of the public sphere—the domain that statistics have historically been designed to quantify. One of the earliest examples of this contrast was the publicity on lynchings in the U.S. South. Although Black women were lynched in numbers, this history dwells largely in the shadows of those Black male victims whose violent deaths were sensationally documented and became a major impetus for the transformation of U.S. race relations (Feimster, 2009). The relevancy of Black men's lynching and the counting of their bodies within the public sphere suggests the state's patriarchal preoccupation with male bodies. Black men, as men, were those whose supposed crimes and subsequent lynchings were rallying points for

White fear and White supremacist governance as well as for Black social struggle.

Today, a similar relationship between the statistics and visibility of Black men and women in the public sphere exists in the conversation on Black incarceration. While Black men are the virtual face of the prison system, the rates for Black women have increased dramatically, where now 1 out of every 100 Black women ages 35–39 is incarcerated compared to 1 out of every 355 White women and 1 out of every 265 for the entire female population (Pew Center on the States, 2008). Similarly, rising HIV rates for Black women echo those of Black men. Black women now account for 66 percent of the new cases of HIV among women, and have the third highest new infection rate, trailing Black and Latino men (Centers for Disease Control and Prevention, 2013). A study from Johns Hopkins University found that Black women in several major East Coast cities are infected at five times the rate of the rest of the country, dramatically paralleling the numbers from some of the hard-hit countries of the African continent (HIV Prevention Trials Network, 2012).

We have strategically turned to statistics here to place the life pictures of Black women into conversation with those of Black men and locate the forces that generate this comparison. Understanding this framework also reveals what statistics do and do not tell about Black women's challenges as well as those of Black men. More recent research illuminates how Black women's crisislike conditions are not as easily quantifiable as those of Black men and are barely visible to the state or in the public sphere. Only in the past decade have the complexities of the social implications of Black women's health disparities and incarceration been the source of research that takes race, class, and gender seriously.[6] Like Black men, Black women find themselves in acute social conditions but are more often read as agents in their difficult circumstances rather than victims of a confining social world. Black women's health and economics are constructed not only as a question of agency but also within the domestic, rather than public, sphere.

While feminists have argued against the split of these two spheres, the production of statistics reaffirms the divide. In their focus on the public sphere, statistics fail to capture in numbers many of the devastating ways Black women experience the intersection of racism, homophobia, heterosexism, and economic poverty, often out of the public eye in the domestic or private sphere. For example, statistics have never dealt with sexual violence against women beginning in slavery and ongoing in the so-called private spaces of domestic labor or conjugal relations. As mentioned, this also includes more general physical violence against Black women historically highlighted by lynchings. Little statistical work has been done to break down the financial demands on women in relation to their children, in child care, feeding and clothing of children, care of elderly dependents, and so on, while demonizing stereotypes of Black women as welfare queens continue to simplify their lives and agency into those of state-dependent drones and deviant matriarchs. The statistics that are produced about Black women tend to be framed as issues of private responsibility and in this way often affirm these persistent stereotypes.

Since its inception, the patriarchic and White supremacist U.S. state has been concerned with the place and control of its riskiest population—its Black chattel and then second-class Black citizens—and it has produced statistics as a mechanism of their governance. As mentioned previously, this interest began as early as the writing of the Constitution in the controversies surrounding counting this country's enslaved population. Contemporaneously, the "statistical panic" (Woodward, 2009) that governs so much of everyday public life, from broken-windows policing strategies to an individual's selection of residential neighborhoods to presidential elections, is based on assumptions about Black males' riskiness made possible by statistics concerning their troubled presence in the public sphere. The nation is inundated and galvanized by statistics of riskiness in the public sphere; statistics on unemployment, crime, incarceration, murder, and premature death abound and are highly publicized. These are the so-called facts that inform Black male riskiness and their at-risk status. It is the primacy of these statistics in the everyday notions of who men of color are that educates popular consent to the coercive practices of the state's extensive security apparatus but also the myriad programs that propose to remediate their at-risk character. In contrast, statistics about Black women in the public sphere are of little notice, in the domestic sphere are lightly collected, and in general are used to pathologize them. Hence, their being at risk is concealed.

No critical analytical lens has been installed by the state or in the public sphere to problemize Black women's conditions by contradicting statistics' claim to truth. Without critical analyses of the structures, in this instance patriarchy, that precondition Black women's and men's struggles (whether statistically demonstrated, newsworthy or not), the lived conditions of Black women and men and all people of color will be very difficult to transform.

Patriarchal Values and Racial Gender Roles

In the United States, women and men of color exist under different social expectations from each other and, most notably, from White women and men. In other words, the zero-sum game, which frames Black women and men together in an olympics of social suffering, does not account for how racial gender roles circumscribe each group differently. Patriarchy, through the widespread belief that it is enacted singularly by men's sexism and control of women, prevents our understanding of it as a force structuring men's lives in multiple ways. The most important of these are the relationships men have with themselves and each other within and across race. These unexplored sites of patriarchy's influence on men's racialized and gendered social roles now guide our analysis.

As an autonomous field of social classification of people in the United States, race is imbued with power that separates, hierarchizes, and influences the reading of bodies. Now refuted on biological terms, race nonetheless continues as a hegemonic grammar for physical difference in U.S. society revolving around such features as skin color, hair, and so on, which also have a set of cultural and social assumptions. These physical notions of race have also shifted into cultural understandings that essentialize and equate Black women and men with Black culture. Rather than viewed as cultur- ally American, Black people are considered practitioners first and foremost of Black culture. A deeply contested notion, Black culture is represented in the Moynihan (1965) report, where it is used to pathologize Black people's economic and social disenfranchisement as symptomatic of a destructive and dysfunctional culture. The reductive understanding of race and its mapping onto culture makes Black people inescapable practitioners of this deficient culture. Ignoring centuries of institutional racism and structural inequality supported by the state, these social narratives and explanations of Black cul- ture present Black culture as abnormal and deficient.

These cultural understandings of race shape women and men differently. The social essentializing of male and female difference occurs at a cultural level between and within racial and ethnic groups. This differentiation is per- tinent because it dictates the social and gendered roles and expectations for men and women of color. For example, Black women and Latinas experience gendered racial and ethnic roles that are different from each other's as well as from those of Black and Latino men. Patriarchal norms create different measures and experiences for men and women of color.

One vantage for observing these differences in patriarchal racial gen- der roles is through stereotypes of men and women of color. Operating at the representational level, racial and ethnic stereotypes articulate the social and cultural norms and assumptions by which racialized bodies are read and understood. They create a differentiation and deviance from the dominant Respectable middle-class White gender roles that are patriarchal and natural- ized as the normative personhood. Illustratively called "controlling images" by Patricia Hill Collins (2000, pp. 69–96), stereotypes, specifically of Black people from enslavement forward, were created by White power structures to justify racial, gender, and class forms of subordination, oppression, and violence. These caricatures frame Black people as embodiments of deviant behavior, thinking and being, in gender-specific ways. Black feminists have criticized the prevailing stereotypes of Black women as mammies, matriarchs, and jezebels, three images among others that construct Black women as subservient and asexual (mammy), domineering and emasculating (matriarch), and hypersexual and sexually irresistible (jezebel). These representations deviate from the patriarchal idealized norms of Respectable White womanhood and femininity that are frail, pure (sexually and morally), and subservient to men. This cult of true White womanhood, as a racialized formation, was unattainable by Black women who in their gendered and racial position were socially and economically vulnerable to sexual violation and unable to embody the social standards set forth by the dominant society; this established Black women as deviant.

Stereotypes also exist for Black men and other men of color, exposing distinct sets of abnormal gendered expectations and roles for these men. Among the most common stereotypes of Black men are the historical Sambo figure and buck that continue to shape the perception of Black men as dullards or criminals. The Sambo stereotype projects images of Black men who are passive, which reinforces dominant patriarchal norms and White male privilege, whereas the stereotype of the threatening Black male is the personification of White patriarchal authority's anxiety. As Frantz Fanon's (1967) work has shown, these stereotypes have always been more informative about White male fear (those in structural and institutional power) than about Black people, and namely, Black men. The same can be said about the gendered racial stereotypes of other groups. The naturalization of White patriarchal authority in the United States enables fear of Black men to be seen as a question of race and gender rather than patriarchal competition, specifically between men. The hegemonic acceptance and longevity of the stereotypes of Black men continue in contemporary representations of Black men as athletes, gangsters, and thugs that evoke the same hypermasculine, hyperviolent, and hypersexual characterizations.

Black women and men, like all racial groups, negotiate the weight of their grossly gendered stereotypes, laboring to defy them, living with them, and in some instances appropriating and embodying them. And yet, their negotiation of these stereotypes requires an engagement with patriarchy in different ways. Limited discussion of patriarchy as something that affects only women enables its effects on the possible social roles for men of color as racialized, gendered, sexual subjects to go unexplored. The gendered positioning of men of color in relationship to that of White men needs to be questioned and transformed. In a White supremacist patriarchy like the United States, men of color, and notably queer men of color, are unable, in spite of the vigor of their misguided efforts to do so, to achieve these normative and naturalized gender and sexual roles because of their economic, racial, and sexual positioning *and* performance. Scholarship on queer Black men and masculinity offers some of the few analyses detailing the heteronormative and homophobic nature of patriarchy and how it affects men of color. In general, however, men of color's investment in patriarchal standpoints and practices continues to support male hierarchical competition and dominance.

Much like stereotypes, statistics on Black men tell us as much about that field of competition, and therefore what is being threatened or at stake, as they do about the circumstances of Black men. These statistics advance what Omi and Winant (1994) label as a racial project that surveils Black and other men of color against the norm of men's gender roles. While not necessarily originating in racist intent, the consequences of the hypervisibility and invisibility of men of color's bodies and actions have racialized effects. As argued previously, in the instance of Black men, their abnormal gender and racial constructions, when read through the tool of statistics, project them not only as an at-risk population but also as a risky population needing social monitoring and control. The metrics of Black men confirm their threat at the same time that they "prove" they are in crisis. In a patriarchal society of hierarchy and domination, non-White men are seen as the competition and threat to White male patriarchal power and are engaged within this framework. Consider the categories most frequently used to create Black men's state of crisis—incarceration, drug possession, unemployment, early death, absent fathers, and so forth. Together, these statistics reveal the problems that patriarchy seeks to discipline, such as the family, governance, and economic markets, through maintenance of masculinist hierarchical power and control. Patriarchal competition and authority mediate the field of legality and illegality, the economic market, and access to resources. It is within this White patriarchal capitalist value structure and the metrics used to sustain it that Black men underperform or fail, are a risk, or are at risk. Without an analysis of patriarchy, the field of competition for men of color is framed around women of color, rather than White men and other men.

Patriarchy, as well as capitalism, orients social relations around competition and a hierarchical ordering system. This framework most forcefully guides men's relationships with each other. Competition is one of the central engines of patriarchal as well as capitalist systems. It energizes the desire to be right and to win, as well as the commonsense logics of "the haves and have-nots" and "different slices of the one pie." These have become naturalized values and pursuits within the social dynamics of labor and the economy and inter- and intrapersonal relationships. Patriarchy as a social current generates male competition for control of external power. As bell hooks (2004) contends, patriarchy teaches that all social relations are power struggles (p. 116). Within this thinking, the goal of competition is mastery, control, and domination in order to establish hierarchy. Human relations, specifically those between men, dynamically exist with this blueprint. Yet, it is critical to note that competition for mastery within patriarchal thinking is gendered and raced. The field of competition constructs different roles and expectations for men and women, and men and women of color alike, because this field possesses a normative construct of White men in competition with each other.

All too often, the framing of comparisons between Black men's and Black women's social conditions, whether in the media or nonfeminist-inspired scholarship, places them in a patriarchal field of competition. Evident in the College Board reports (College Board, 2010; Lee & Ransom, 2011) and statistics more broadly is a competitive field that drives dichotomous readings, which in turn isolate winners and losers, failures and successes. For example, Black women are not just points of comparison for Black men, but their successes are points of comparison for Black men's failures. This juxtaposition, demonstrated through the metrics of education and employment, ironically supports White male patriarchal systems rather than contests them. Yet, Black women's supposedly aberrant gender roles as matriarchs challenge patriarchal values, and, therefore, they are simultaneously criticized for their impact on the Black family. Black women's social achievement is framed and blamed as destroying the Black family. At the same time, White racial hierarchy operates in such a way that Black women's advancement over Black men is not seen as threatening the White establishment in the way that Black men's often does. By placing Black men and women in the same comparative and competitive frame, race is confirmed as the salient common denominator in their social and economic disadvantages. Their gender differences disavowed, these analyses fail to identify how patriarchal forces shape the roles Black men and women are expected to fill.

Wahneema Lubiano (1992) recharacterizes this juxtaposition of Black men and women as functioning as a dyad of "hero" and "outlaw" (p. 337) and their roles as less of competition than of dependency. She pointedly asks, "So what is going to destroy America? Black welfare queens in particular and Black female misbehavior in general" (p. 340). This tongue-in-cheek and ironic response evokes the damned-if-you-do-or-don't condition that Black women experience differently from Black men. Lubiano frames the racial patriarchal hierarchical field where racial difference distracts from the larger patriarchal plane that monitors women and observes the competition between men. Black women buffer White patriarchal models of Black men's failures.

Competition for power, centered on the external control of bodies and resources, illustrates the overlapping value structures embedded in racial patriarchal thinking and the forms of competition for resources and individual gain that are the operating notions of a capitalist market and economy. Racial difference establishes the historic parameters of the control of bodies, their hierarchies of people, and access to resources. This system of competition, naturalized by patriarchy itself, has hindered men's social relations from being reconstructed around different forms of relating.

As hooks (2004) contends, competition is the framework in which patriarchal male identity (the dominant notion available) is produced. Men's self-worth is constructed through the patriarchal tenets of the ability and capacity not only to dominate women but to gain more control and authority within the male hierarchy. One's sense of worth and self is defined through external actions and demonstrations of power as well as an internal system of control and mastery of self and others. Within a patriarchal paradigm of masculine power, one's power is built and exercised through the control of one's self, one's urges, emotions, and mind, in addition to things external. This power base is also defined in opposition to those qualities associated with the feminine such as emotion, vulnerability, and this perceived loss of control associated with the sentient body. The implications are that one's manhood, male identity, the masculine status naturalized and limited through this mode of thinking, is reduced to these forms of control. One's failure to master, to successfully compete, or to achieve external power in the form of control of resources or of others can be transformed into a dearth of personal worth or value as well as an inference of femininity. Pascoe (2007) ethnographically documents that with young predominantly White men, this failure to perform patriarchal masculinity often turned into homophobic disciplining, while she also observed that young Black men scrutinized one another's masculinity through their proximities to cultural Whiteness. Numerous scholars have examined in school environments how young Black men's "acting White" or performance of racial cultural norms shapes their relationships with their peers and academic achievement (Fordham & Ogbu, 1986; Harper, 2006; Ogbu, 2004). They have also examined the (limited) types of masculinities available to young Black men and how, in turn, they operate in relation to these paradigms (Connell, 1993; Harper, 2004). These constrictions are in large part what makes the narrative of crisis's call for role modeling such a problem. Much like the Moynihan (1965) report, the call for patriarchal manhood goes unchallenged, and the forces that perpetuate it, obscured and unaddressed. Men are asked to build a sense of self and a mode of being around a skill set that allows for more successful competition for mastery, control, and power. An internal world of self-control is arid soil in which to nurture a rich and intricate sense of self. This brief theorization is not intended to oversimplify what is an extremely complicated and engrained system of social influence and thinking nor to undervalue its impacts. By contrast, it offers some of the key modes through which patriarchy operates, and these are in need of deeper exploration in research and intervention agendas for young men of color.

Only recently has the social structuring of gender roles expanded to allow women to operate in this field of competition in the public sphere. Women now vie with each other and with men for hierarchical power and status. How women live and operate in the patriarchal field of competition needs greater analysis. By virtue of their female body, status, and expectations of dominant feminine characteristics, women do not benefit from patriarchy in the same way men do. Similarly, intersecting racial, classed, and sexual hierarchies influence men's abilities to achieve benefits and status even as they invest in competing for patriarchal power. While this has been readily observed, politicized, and critiqued by the feminist movement writ large, patriarchy's naturalization on its impacts on women has foreclosed deeper investigation and analysis of the implications of competition on men.

Calling attention to how male competition operates within patriarchy begins to denaturalize its system of order, value structure, and orientation, whereby men's struggles can be better understood. We ask: How is competition among men taught and learned by young men of color in the classroom, through parenting, in the social field, and in employment? What are the differences in experiences of competition between men and women? How do young men of color experience winning, losing, being right and wrong, and control? How do differences in access to capital structure the ability of men of color to compete for masculine status? These are some of the questions that reorient the differentiated impacts of patriarchy. We take up this exploration through the consideration of Black male Respectability.

Patriarchy and Respectability

The male mastery over self, other men, and women and children that racial patriarchy demands of "real" men is normed by rules that align it with the functioning of the institutions of our meritocratic capitalist society. Respectability, as a cultural form of patriarchy, is the province of middle-aged and older middle- and upper-class heterosexual men who establish, or at least strive for, mastery in the private and public institutions of society. The most readily identifiable form of male patriarchic Respectability is paternal male dominant authority in the domestic sphere, particularly over members of nuclear family units whose material needs Respectable men control and provide for. Respectable men enact their dominance as leaders, providers, and protectors of nuclear family units. Their obligatory normative heterosexual identities are made evident by their positions as husbands to their wives and as fathers of their children, in control of the sexuality and sexual expression of the female members of those family units, and as patriarchic models for their sons.

Middle-class Respectability also involves male mastery of the self. Respectable men are in control of their emotions, they are rational, proactive, independent, and heterosexual. All these attributes are understood to require personal control of the baser human or immoral impulses, many of which are associated with femininity and women.

We argued previously that patriarchy also involves relationships of competition for mastery among men. Masculine status in a patriarchy is calculated through dominance over, and through leadership of, other men in the public sphere. It is exercised through competition for dominance in the formal institutions of civil society: economic, religious, social, and political. A Respectable man with high masculine status is one who has achieved that status through competition with other men and is upwardly mobile through the hierarchies of such institutions. In our capitalist society such mastery is often demonstrated through ostentatious material ownership and consumption. State-sanctioned coercive violence is also a provenance of male Respectability. The police, border patrol, and military are all bastions of male Respectable patriarchy. Respectability is a male cultural form associated with White middle-class men but practiced across racial groups.

Cliff Huxtable from the iconic *The Cosby Show* (Weinberger, Leeson, & Sandrich, 1984) is the quintessential model of such a high-status Black Respectable man as summed up in the following exchange with his TV son, Theo. He aptly demonstrates the public and private sphere elements of male Respectable patriarchy.

Theo: But maybe I was born to be a regular person and have a regular life. If you weren't a doctor, I wouldn't love you less, because you're my dad. So rather than feeling disappointed because I'm not like you, maybe you should accept who I am and love me anyway, because I'm your son.

Cliff: Theo . . . that's the dumbest thing I've ever heard in my life! No wonder you get Ds in everything! . . . Now I'm telling you, you are going to try as hard as you can. And you're going to do it because I said so. I am your father. I brought you into this world, and I'll take you out!

Clearly there are serious problems of inequity and injustice in these practices of Respectable masculinity. The tensions and contradictions in a society where democratic and egalitarian values are discursively hegemonic are legion. Importantly, Respectability places serious restrictions on the range of acceptable masculine practices, marking as deviant a wide range of possibilities outside its narrow view. Nevertheless, Respectable masculinity is the norm, and Respectable men like Cliff Huxtable and, for that matter, Barack Obama are the commonly accepted models for masculine performance and status among both Black and White people in the United States. There are, however, differential impacts on differently positioned peoples.

Unfortunately, for men of color in general and Black men in particular, the achievement of masculine status through patriarchic Respectability requires economic, social, and cultural capital. Paternal dominance presupposes the possession of the capital to form and sustain a middle-class nuclear family in which the man is the provider and protector. It also presupposes the capital necessary to get a decent formal education and mobilize the social networks and economic capital necessary to be upwardly mobile in formal institutions. To use the Huxtable example, Cliff somehow had to accumulate the cultural capital and mobilize the social networks necessary to work his way through the hierarchies of educational institutions to get his degree and become a medical doctor. He then works his way up through this profession, mobilizing his cultural and social capital, to become economically successful. All through this process he was in successful competition for various kinds of scarce resources with other men. This journey required large quantities of economic capital and also produced at the end of the process sufficient economic capital for forms of ownership and consumption that mark him as a high-status Respectable man. This capital also allows him to form and dominate a nuclear family of which he is the protector, provider, and leader, in other words, the dominant figure, the Respectable patriarch.

Most men of color, however, because of the workings of racism and economic exploitation, find it very difficult to accumulate sufficient quantities of cultural, social, and economic capital to produce Respectable masculine status for themselves. This is particularly true for young men of color, because in addition to the disadvantages of White supremacist racism and economic poverty, they have not had the time to accumulate the cultural and social capital necessary to be Respectable. In these circumstances, they seek other means of creating a masculine status for themselves.

In U.S. society, patriarchy is the grammar of masculine status. We have seen this clearly in what might be termed *the benign patriarchy of the Respectable Huxtable*. For those men who for reasons of class oppression and racism do not have the capital to be Respectable, there is an alternative cultural form of masculinity and status based on the same patriarchic grammar as Respectability that we will term *Reputation* (Wilson, 1995). In this cultural form of patriarchic masculine practice, men dominate women outside the institution of marriage. They accomplish this by being successful with women, having multiple sexual partners, and often, children with multiple women, thereby demonstrating their dominance through control of their women's sexuality, their own reproductive prowess, their heterosexuality, virility, and, in sum, their masculine status.

Reputational masculine status, much like Respectable status, is also established through dominance over and through competition with male peers. However, in the case of Reputation, such dominance is competitively accomplished outside the formal institutions of civil society, through physical violence, antiauthoritarian practices, criminal bravado, athletic contests, verbal bouts, music and dance performance, and so on. Conspicuous material consumption and display can also be important. Expensive cars, clothes, and jewelry as well as generosity in peer groups all are signs of Reputational masculine status.

Snoop Dogg (2001) on his iconic album *Doggystyle* is a quintessential model of a high-status Black Reputational male. Throughout the album, he clearly demonstrates the construction of Reputational male status through the domination of women by controlling and exploiting their sexuality and through competition with and domination of other men through violence, antiauthoritarian practice, and material ostentation.

Reputational Snoop Dogg is the Janus face of Respectable Huxtable: young/middle aged, urban/suburban, poor/middle class, uneducated/educated, Black English/standard English, unmarried/married, successful in informal institutions/successful in formal institutions. What they have in common, however, is high masculine status achieved on the basis of patriarchic mastery, dominance of women, and competition with other men.

It should be obvious that male Reputational practice impedes educational achievement for young men of color. Academic success is generally not relevant to the creation of masculine status within peer groups that produce Reputational masculine status. Educational success also requires acceptance of Respectable standards of male status achievement understood as unachievable. Reputational male practice produces disciplinary and authority issues for practicing men of color while it fuels existing White prejudices and lowers teacher expectations as it reinforces societal stereotypes.

However, Respectable male practice has embedded in it the imperative of mastery of self. This can have adverse effects on academic performance, especially for Black men and men of color whose quest for Respectable male status is threatened by capital deficiencies. Here the need to not display vulnerability and the urge toward individualism leaves them ill equipped to use the resources and techniques mobilized by women and others to maximize their educational achievement. Moreover, the impetus to competition among Respectable men may well work against Black men and other men of color who are described as simultaneously at risk and risky in all academic settings dominated by White men.

Conclusion: Patriarchy and a New Conceptual Framework

One of the overarching points of this chapter is that redressing the outstanding issues facing young men of color requires a more comprehensive investigation of the value systems, roles, and perspectives orienting and training them. Through exploring patriarchy, we contend that we gain greater insight into the types of gender roles and social expectations that are central to the social phenomena of crisis currently witnessed. Analyses of the intersecting racial and classed dimensions of patriarchal power can clarify the distinct experiences of gender for men and women of color. Feminist and intersectional analyses have deepened women's understandings of gender roles, identity, and their relationships to dominant (patriarchal) constructions of femininity. Women in turn have used this critical consciousness to explore, expand, and express diversified notions of womanhood and femininity, including their own masculinity. Although the analytical tools of feminism were designed for all, patriarchal interpretations of their functions previously discussed have constrained their reach and deployment by men. Critical analyses of male gender roles, as we have argued, are needed to expose their current patriarchal assumptions and the complicated ways they simultaneously constrain and benefit men. Deeper analyses of patriarchy's force in structuring the lives and identities of men are our most urgent recommendation.

Our emphasis on patriarchy within a conceptual framework of racism and economic inequality creates a new approach and generates new sets of responses. At a practical level, this method or framework suggests considering how patriarchy and its articulation with race and economics influences all parts of the educational experience of young people, from teachers to students to institutions. How are patriarchal notions fostered in the curricula and pedagogy of teachers? How are they then imparted and learned in the classroom? How do institutional practices generate and reinforce patriarchal values and structures? High schools, colleges, and universities are not separate from society or the families in which patriarchal, racial, and classed perspectives play out in different but no less influential ways. Thus, transforming our educational institutions remains a critical, but only partial, component in shifting the experience of young men and women of color. Mapping this terrain will move the conversation around these unsolvable and crisislike problems away from a personalized focus on young men of color and their communities toward the sociocultural and political economic analysis outlined in this chapter.

While patriarchal values are still dominant, there are alternative orientations. Our response to the emphasis on competition previously discussed is collaboration and dialogue, modeled in the very writing of and approach to this chapter. Framing issues of men of color in a constructive relationship with those of women of color means looking at the problems from a shared space of care and recognition, identifying their different and mutual challenges, and addressing them from a collaborative and interconnected framework. As we have argued, patriarchal orientations have made it difficult for men to conceptualize women except as oppositional and part of the hierarchical competition that underlies men's relationships with themselves and each other. Further exploration into men's dynamics writ large would help clarify the operations of patriarchy. They may also uncover how these vantages and structures are resisted, exposing how men already are creating and participating in more egalitarian forms of socialization, relating and building connection as well as divesting themselves of patriarchal power. These practices and perspectives hold the potential to become foundational practices for new masculinities and gender sociality.

This investigation must also continue to explore patriarchy's influence on women from this more expanded conceptualization. For example, as discussed in this chapter, women are often found to be high performing in the educational system, and yet, beyond matriculation and graduation rates, we ask: How are patriarchal values shaping women's lives and experiences in unconsidered or more covert ways? A 2011 study at Princeton University found that in spite of women's acceleration and achievement at the university level, women do not assume leadership positions to the same degree or with the same conviction as men ("Report of the Steering Committee on Undergraduate Women's Leadership," 2013). These findings beg questions about the culture of leadership's relationship to patriarchy, including the process of its pursuit and the expectations for how it is executed and what can be experienced. Examining leadership through our conceptual framework is a starting point for investigating the broader scope of patriarchal influences in the educational system and how patriarchy extends into the workforce and political and social fields, shaping outcomes for men and women. More research is needed about the types of values cultivated in education and their long-standing impacts on the life trajectories of women and men.

The more encompassing lines of inquiry introduced in this chapter diverge from the College Board's reports (College Board, 2010; Lee & Ransom, 2011) and the standard academic and popular practices that place the conditions of men and women of color at odds with one another. Deepening our understandings about the challenges facing young men of color is a process of recognizing and addressing how they reflect larger visions of gender, race, equality, and difference. Why not research and write a companion volume on patriarchy, gender roles, and women's achievement in addition to one that addresses women and men of color's achievement in unison? We believe that the much-written-about gender gap may in fact be a more fruitful basis to explore how patriarchy generates the paradigms used to frame how we think about men and women, gender difference, and social relations at large.

Notes

1. Our use of *Respectability* names a patriarchal understanding of the notion of respect that we differentiate from the popular usages of the term. This patriarchal conceptualization stems from Peter Wilson's (1995) ethnographic analysis of the gender and classed values of Respectability and Reputation orienting social relations on the Caribbean island of Providencia, and E. T. Gordon's (1997) retheorization of the values within the framework of Black culture and Black masculinity in the United States.

2. Historically in the patriarchal social framework of the United States, culturally associated feminine qualities such as emotionality and gentleness have been essentialized as women's nature, cultivated in women and discouraged in men, and broadly viewed in opposition to the qualities of the masculine constructed as inherent to men. While we discuss the patriarchal investment and essentializing of such values as competition, domination, and hierarchy as masculine, other cultural associations with the masculine are rationality, linearity, and strength.

3. This reference elucidates the forces that generate the particular emasculating stereotypes that men of Asian descent confront and are targeted with in the West. For a sample of readings on Asian American stereotyping and subjectivity in the United States, see Eng (2001), Lowe (1996), and Shimizu (2007, 2012).

4. W. E. B. Du Bois's (1899/1995) *The Philadelphia Negro* is one of the first pieces of scholarship documenting the economically and socially

challenging conditions of urban Black people that would later become quantified in the language of *crisis*.

5. For more in-depth consideration of statistics and their evolving use by the U.S. government before and after the Depression see Anderson (1988, pp. 159–190) and Duncan and Shelton (1978, pp. 23–29).

6. For a novel approach to the massive health disparities between Black women and women of other racial groups, see Geronimus (2001).

References

Alexander-Floyd, N. G. (2007). *Gender, race, and nationalism in contemporary Black politics*. New York, NY: Palgrave Macmillan.

Anderson, M. J. (1988). *The American census: A social history.* New Haven, CT: Yale University Press.

Banks, R. R. (2011). *Is marriage for White people? How the African American marriage decline affects everyone*. New York, NY: Dutton.

Benhabib, S. (1992). Models of public space: Hannah Arendt, the liberal tradition, and Jürgen Habermas. In C. Calhoun (Ed.), *Habermas and the public sphere* (pp. 73–98). Cambridge, MA: MIT Press.

Benhabib, S. (1993). Feminist theory and Hannah Arendt's concept of the public space. *History of the Human Sciences, 6*(2), 97–115.

Brown, A. L. (2011). Same old stories: The Black male in social science and educational literature, 1930s to the present. *Teachers College Record, 113*(9), 2047–2079.

Brown, A. L., & Donnor, J. K. (2011). Toward a new narrative on Black males, education, and public policy. *Race Ethnicity and Education, 14*(1), 17–32.

Butler, J. (1993). *Bodies that matter: On the discursive limits of "sex."* New York, NY: Routledge.

Butler, J. (2004). *Undoing gender*. New York, NY: Routledge.

Centers for Disease Control and Prevention. (2013). *HIV incidence*. Retrieved April 20, 2012, from http://www.cdc.gov/hiv/topics/surveillance/incidence.htm

Clarke, A. Y. (2011). *Inequalities of love: College-educated Black women and the barriers to romance and family*. Durham, NC: Duke University Press.

College Board. (2010). *The educational crisis facing young men of color: Reflections on four days of dialogue on the educational challenges of minority males*. New York, NY: College Board Advocacy & Policy Center.

Collins, P. H. (2000). *Black feminist thought: Knowledge, consciousness, and the politics of empowerment* (2nd ed.). New York, NY: Routledge.

Combahee River Collective. (1977). *The Combahee River Collective statement*. Retrieved July 15, 2012, from http://circuitous.org/scraps/combahee.html

Connell, R. W. (1993). Disruptions: Improper masculinities and schooling. In L. Weis & M. Fine (Eds.), *Beyond silenced voices* (pp. 191–208). Albany, NY: SUNY Press.

Connell, R. W., & Messerschmidt, J. W. (2005). Hegemonic masculinity: Rethinking the concept. *Gender & Society, 19*(6), 829–859.

Crenshaw, K. (1991). Mapping the margins: Intersectionality, identity politics, and violence against women of color. *Stanford Law Review, 43*(6), 1241–1299.

Desrosières, A. (1998). *The politics of large numbers: A history of statistical reasoning.* Cambridge, MA: Harvard University Press.

Dogg, S. (2001). *Doggystyle* [CD]. Los Angeles, CA: Death Row Records.

Drake, S. C., & Cayton, H. R. (1970). *Black metropolis: A study of Negro life in a northern city.* New York, NY: Harcourt, Brace & World.

Du Bois, W. E. B. (1995). *The Philadelphia Negro: A social study.* Philadelphia: University of Pennsylvania Press. (Original work published 1899)

Duncan, J. W., & Shelton, W. C. (1978). *Revolution in United States government statistics, 1926–1976.* Washington, DC: U.S. Department of Commerce, Office of Federal Statistical Policy and Standards.

Eng, D. L. (2001). *Racial castration: Managing masculinity in Asian America.* Durham, NC: Duke University Press.

Fanon, F. (1967). *Black skin, White masks.* New York, NY: Grove Press.

Fausto-Sterling, A. (2000). *Sexing the body: Gender politics and the construction of sexuality.* New York, NY: Basic Books.

Feimster, C. N. (2009). *Southern horrors: Women and the politics of rape and lynching.* Cambridge, MA: Harvard University Press.

Feinberg, L. (2003). *Stone butch blues.* New York, NY: Alyson Books.

Ferguson, A. (2001). *Bad boys: Public schools in the making of Black masculinity.* Ann Arbor: University of Michigan Press.

Fordham, S., & Ogbu, J. U. (1986). Black students' school success: Coping with the "burden of 'acting White.'" *Urban Review, 18*(3), 176–206.

Fraser, N. (1990). Rethinking the public sphere: A contribution to the critique of actually existing democracy. *Social Text, 25*(26), 56–80.

Frazier, E. F. (1997). *Black bourgeoisie.* New York, NY: Free Press Paperbacks.

Geronimus, A. T. (2001). Understanding and eliminating racial inequalities in women's health in the United States: The role of the weathering conceptual framework. *Journal of the American Medical Women's Association, 56*(4), 133–136.

Gordon, E. T. (1997). Cultural politics of Black masculinity. *Transforming Anthropology, 6*(1/2), 36–53.

Gordon, E. T., Gordon, E. W., & Nembhard, J. G. G. (1994). Social science literature concerning African American men. *The Journal of Negro Education, 63*(4), 508–531.

Habermas, J. (1991). *The structural transformation of the public sphere: An inquiry into a category of bourgeois society.* Cambridge, MA: MIT Press.

Hacking, I. (1991). How should we do the history of statistics? In G. Burchell, C. Gordon, & P. Miller (Eds.), *The Foucault effect: Studies in governmentality* (pp. 181–196). Chicago, IL: University of Chicago Press.

Halberstam, J. (1998). *Female masculinity.* Durham, NC: Duke University Press.

Harper, S. R. (2004). The measure of a man: Conceptualizations of masculinity among high-achieving African American male college students. *Berkeley Journal of Sociology, 48*(1), 89–107.

Harper, S. R. (2006). Peer support for African American male college achievement: Beyond internalized racism and the burden of "acting White." *The Journal of Men's Studies, 14*(3), 337–358.

Harris-Perry, M. (2011). *Sister citizen: Shame, stereotypes, and Black women in America*. New Haven, CT: Yale University Press.

Hartman, S. V. (1997). *Scenes of subjection: Terror, slavery, and self-making in nineteenth-century America*. New York, NY: Oxford University Press.

HIV Prevention Trials Network. (2012). *HIV rates for Black women in parts of the US much higher than previously estimated*. Retrieved April 20, 2012, from http://www .hptn.org/web%20documents/IndexDocs/064ISIS_PressRelease8Mar2012.pdf

hooks, b. (1990). *Yearning: Race, gender, and cultural politics*. Cambridge, MA: South End Press.

hooks, b. (2004). *The will to change: Men, masculinity, and love*. New York, NY: Washington Square Press.

Jackman, M. R. (1994). *The velvet glove: Paternalism and conflict in gender, class, and race relations*. Berkeley: University of California Press.

Johnson, C. S. (1967). *Growing up in the Black belt: Negro youth in the rural South*. New York, NY: Schocken Books.

Lee, J. M., & Ransom, T. (2011). *The educational experience of young men of color: A review of research, pathways and progress*. New York, NY: College Board Advocacy & Policy Center.

Legette, W. (1999). The crisis of the Black male: A new ideology in Black politics. In A. Reed, Jr. (Ed.), *Without justice for all: The new liberalism and our retreat from racial equality* (pp. 291–324). Boulder, CO: Westview Press.

Lewis, A. E. (2003). *Race in the schoolyard: Negotiating the color line in classrooms and communities*. Piscataway, NJ: Rutgers University Press.

Lowe, L. (1996). *Immigrant acts: On Asian American cultural politics*. Durham, NC: Duke University Press.

Lubiano, W. (1992). Black ladies, welfare queens and state minstrels: Ideological war by narrative means. In T. Morrison (Ed.), *Race-ing justice, en-gendering power: Essays on Anita Hill, Clarence Thomas, and the construction of social reality* (pp. 323–363). New York, NY: Pantheon Books.

Moynihan, D. P. (1965). *The Negro family: The case for national action*. Retrieved November 9, 2012, from http://www.dol.gov/oasam/programs/history/webid -meynihan.htm#.UJ1Pz4XgKb8

National Women's Law Center. (2011). *Poverty among women and families, 2000–2010: Extreme poverty reaches record levels as Congress faces critical choices*. Retrieved April 8, 2013, from http://www.nwlc.org/sites/default/files/pdfs/povertyamongwomen andfamilies2010final.pdf

Nitsche, N., & Brueckner, H. (2009). *Opting out of the family? Social change in racial inequality in family formation patterns and marriage outcomes among highly educated women*. Retrieved April 17, 2012, from http://www.yale.edu/ciqle/Nitsche _brueckner_Executive%20summary.pdf

Noguera, P. A. (2008). *The trouble with Black boys: . . . And other reflections on race, equity, and the future of public education*. San Francisco, CA: Jossey-Bass.

Ogbu, J. U. (2004). Collective identity and the burden of "acting White" in Black history, community, and education. *Urban Review, 36*(1), 1–35.

Omi, M., & Winant, H. (1994). *Racial formation in the United States: From the 1960s to the 1990s*. New York, NY: Routledge.

Pascoe, C. J. (2007). *Dude, you're a fag: Masculinity and sexuality in high school.* Berkeley: University of California Press.

Pateman, C. (1988). *The sexual contract.* Cambridge, UK: Polity Press.

Petty, S. W. (1888). *Essays on mankind and political arithmetic.* London, UK: Cassell.

Pew Center on the States. (2008). *One in 100: Behind bars in America 2008.* Retrieved July 16, 2012, from http://www.pewstates.org/uploadedFiles/PCS_Assets/2008/one%20in%20100.pdf

Porter, T. M. (1986). *The rise of statistical thinking, 1820–1900.* Princeton, NJ: Princeton University Press.

Radford-Hill, S. (2000). *Further to fly: Black women and the politics of empowerment.* Minneapolis: University of Minnesota Press.

Report of the Steering Committee on Undergraduate Women's Leadership. (2013). Retrieved September 19, 2013, from http://www.princeton.edu/reports/2011/leadership/

Rios, V. M. (2011). *Punished: Policing the lives of Black and Latino boys.* New York, NY: NYU Press.

Robinson, C. (2000). *Black Marxism: The making of the Black radical tradition.* Chapel Hill: University of North Carolina Press.

Sedgwick, E. K. (1995). "Gosh, Boy George, you must be awfully secure in your masculinity!" In M. Berger, B. Wallis, & S. Watson (Eds.), *Constructing masculinity* (pp. 11–20). New York, NY: Routledge.

Shimizu, C. P. (2007). *The hypersexuality of race: Performing Asian/American women on screen and scene.* Durham, NC: Duke University Press.

Shimizu, C. P. (2012). *Straitjacket sexualities: Unbinding Asian American manhoods in the movies.* Stanford, CA: Stanford University Press.

UC Berkeley Labor Center. (2013). *Annual report: Black employment and unemployment in 2012.* Retrieved April 4, 2013, from http://laborcenter.berkeley.edu/blackworkers/Black_Employment_and_Unemployment_2012.pdf

Weinberger, E., Leeson, M. (Writers), & Sandrich, J. (Director). (1984). Theo's economic lesson [Television series episode]. In M. Carsey & T. Werner (Producers), *The Cosby Show.* New York, NY: National Broadcasting Company.

Williams, E. (1994). *Capitalism and slavery.* Chapel Hill: University of North Carolina Press. (Original work published 1944)

Wilson, P. (1995). *Crab antics: A Caribbean study of the conflict between reputation and respectability.* Long Grove, IL: Waveland Press.

Woodward, K. (2009). *Statistical panic: Cultural politics and poetics of the emotions.* Durham, NC: Duke University Press.

Zuberi, T. (2001). *Thicker than blood: How racial statistics lie.* Minneapolis: University of Minnesota Press.

INTERSECTIONALITY

Robert T. Teranishi and Loni Bordoloi Pazich

This chapter discusses the need for, and challenges associated with, understanding intersectionality relative to race and gender for minority male racial subgroups. The primary concern of the chapter is the treatment of minority male subgroups as aggregate populations and the need for research that addresses the heterogeneity among Asian American and Pacific Islander (AAPI) males. We demonstrate that an intersectional perspective raises awareness about AAPI male subgroups that experience significant inequity, which is too often concealed when they are grouped within the larger population. We begin with a discussion of the normative construction of race and the implications of that framing for the AAPI community. The section that follows introduces the concept of intersectionality as a theoretical frame to understand the confluence of race and gender for AAPI students. Then, using data from the U.S. Census Bureau, we describe the heterogeneity in the AAPI population to represent differences in educational attainment, which varies by ethnicity and gender within the population. We discuss implications for framing and understanding other minority groups and conclude with implications for researchers, policymakers, and practitioners.

"Many of the experiences Black women face are not subsumed within the traditional boundaries of race or gender discrimination as these boundaries are currently understood. . . . The intersection of racism and sexism factors into Black women's lives in ways that cannot be captured wholly by looking at the race or gender dimensions of those experiences separately" (Crenshaw, 1989, p. 1244). In reflecting on the disenfranchisement of Black women,

Kimberlé Crenshaw points to the complicated nature of understanding the effects of race and gender on the educational experiences and outcomes of individuals. Indeed, various aspects of identity are not equally experienced across groups, nor do they necessarily act independently of one another (Delgado & Stefanic, 2012). Forms of oppression related to race, ethnicity, class, gender, and sexual orientation, among other aspects of identity, can independently and collectively confer unique forms of oppression and sub-ordination (Crenshaw, 1989, 1991). While it is important to untangle how race or gender can be separately disadvantaging factors, it is also important to recognize how race and gender, among other aspects of identity, can have a cumulative and compounding effect.

The primary concern of this chapter is the treatment of minority male subgroups as aggregate populations and the need for research that recognizes the heterogeneity within these groups, that is, the differences that exist in and between Black males, Latino males, Native American males, or AAPI males. We focus on AAPI males as a case in point, while offering a theoretical framing that is applicable to other minority male subpopulations.

A focused discussion on AAPI male subgroups is important for the AAPI community for at least three reasons. First, the discourse on race in America often positions AAPI males in a way that does not recognize their unique needs and challenges; in many cases, they are simply omitted from a broader discussion on race relations in America. Second, the AAPI male population is often underserved, which is a particular problem for the subgroups that are experiencing significant educational challenges. Finally, an empirical perspective is needed on the AAPI male population, whose treatment is often driven by assumptions and stereotypes. Responding to the combination of these challenges is important because of the difficulties they raise for effectively representing the needs of AAPI males in the context of research, practice, and community advocacy.

This chapter responds to these shortcomings by demonstrating that an intersectional perspective raises awareness about AAPI male subgroups that experience significant inequity, which is too often concealed when they are grouped within the larger population.

AAPI Males and Normative Constructs of Race and Gender

It is instructive to position the educational experiences and outcomes of AAPI males in a broader understanding of normative constructions of race and gender, as is the case for any other racialized and gendered group. Race and gender are concepts that exist through, and have meaning because of, differences between groups. The differences between groups when it comes to status attainment and other social indicators largely define the social boundaries of race and gender. These differences raise concerns among sociologists—the causes and consequences of racial stratification in our society and the conditions that result in opportunities and mobility for different groups—and make comparative research on racial inequality essential to social science. Thus, cross-sectional research is commonly used to reach conclusions about the relative differences that exist between groups, with between-group differences used to draw inferences about any particular group.

As Gordon and Henery discuss in Chapter 1, the experiences, outcomes, and representation of racial minority groups are defined by the social position of the White majority, its normative position of privilege. On the other end of the racial spectrum, Blacks have historically defined the minority experience in America. Taken together, the Black/White paradigm is the most commonly applied approach to understanding inequality, which often results in the conclusion that problems related to race in American society are dichotomous. In addition to positioning Blacks as inferior along this spectrum, the dichotomous framing places AAPIs, along with Latinos and Native Americans, in vicarious and problematic positions that are difficult to represent in the racial context (Chang, Witt-Sandis, & Hakuta, 1999).

The normative racial construction of AAPIs has been reduced to a stubbornly persistent frame as a model minority. It is not uncommon to read in mainstream media how AAPIs are perceived as the most successful, affluent, and even happiest racial group (Pew Research Center, 2012). While the perception of AAPIs as a successful minority group is deeply engrained in the American ethos, the idea of the model minority is not new. In fact, the proclamation of AAPIs as the model minority is approaching its 50th anniversary. The December 1966 issue of *U.S. News & World Report* published an article titled "Success Story of One Minority Group in U.S." (1966) that proclaimed, "At a time when Americans are awash in worry over the plight of racial minorities, one such minority is winning wealth and respect by dint of its own hard work—not from a welfare check." This article helped to solidify an idea that was presented just a few years earlier by journalist William Petersen (1966), who described Asian Americans as a racial group that had achieved success in the United States despite many obstacles. Two additional mainstream news stories also furthered the idea of the model minority in the minds of Americans: one in *Newsweek* touted that Asians are "outwhiting the Whites" ("Success Story: Outwhiting the Whites," 1971), while the other in *Time* declared that Asians are "the new whiz kids" (Brand, 1987). In a *New York Times* column in 2006 titled "The Model Students," the writer said that "stellar academic achievement has an Asian face" and that others would be "fools" not to learn from these "perfect" students (Kristof, 2006, p. WK13).

Indeed, the image of the model minority is alive and well at the beginning of the new millennium.

In many cases, the dichotomous framing of race results in AAPIs' being used as a wedge group in research, policy, and practice pertaining to racial inequality. For example, the issue of underachievement among minority males is often not viewed as relevant for AAPI males, who are regularly seen as experiencing outcomes comparable to those of White males. As a result, AAPIs are selectively included in minority male discourse to make a point about the relative disadvantage of other minority groups (i.e., a population to serve as a reference point for comparison with the needs of others). Thus, AAPIs are positioned in debates about racial stratification in U.S. society to support or refute the interests of others as part of a larger phenomenon of interest convergence (Bell, 1987), which is characterized by the interests of minority groups being furthered when their interests also align with those of the dominant group. The racial positioning of AAPIs obscures the ways ethnic subgroups' challenges are hidden from view, which we further examine in the section that follows.

In addition to the challenges associated with the racial paradigm, a gendered perspective on AAPIs further complicates an understanding of the experiences of AAPI males. For example, despite the assertion that the educational achievements of AAPI males are equivalent to those of White males, the ways AAPIs are perceived by society are quite different. In fact, while men as a whole are typically viewed as more assertive, aggressive, and masculine, AAPI men are stereotyped as quiet, introverted, and apologetic (Lee & Kumashiro, 2005; Lei, 2003). While this is a departure from the depiction of the typical White male—the normative group—the gendered perception of AAPI men is a particular departure from the depiction of Black, Latino, and Native American men who are often perceived as hypermasculine and overly aggressive. AAPI men also have the added burden of being perceived as unacculturated, perpetual foreigners whose interests are aligned with their country of origin, a depiction that often limits upward mobility to positions of authority and leadership because of fears of disloyalty (Lee & Zia, 2002).[1] Thus, while AAPIs are often used as a population to advance the interests of Whites, the model minority myth does not give them the full benefits and privileges of Whiteness; rather, the model minority myth maintains them as an inferior group.

In this chapter, we explore these issues in the context of education where the dominant perception of AAPIs seldom has a gendered distinction. On the contrary, the perception is overwhelmingly that AAPI men and women have a great deal of parity in educational attainment relative to other racial groups. Accordingly, the following discussion uses an intersectional framework to analyze and present gendered distinctions among AAPIs, with a focus on the educational mobility and outcomes of AAPI males.

The Need to Capture the Complexity of Intersectionality

The concept of intersectionality is a useful tool for capturing the interplay and impact of various strands of identity relative to gauging the stratification of opportunities and outcomes for AAPI males. Using intersectionality as a frame to examine subordination and discrimination is important for AAPIs because, as discussed earlier, their representation is limited by the more common frames for understanding race in America. An intersectional perspective can transcend the prevailing idea that AAPI males are a monolithic and universally successful group with respect to education, a perspective that overlooks the extent to which the AAPI population is very diverse, comprising many cultures, histories, languages, and religions. More important to this chapter, an intersectional frame provides a perspective that can help analyze the ways gender functions differentially across various AAPI subgroups, which transcends the narrow model minority perspective on AAPIs that treats all subgroups as a monolithic and homogeneous whole.

Disaggregated data on the AAPI population reveal a wide range of demographic characteristics that are unlike those of any other racial group in America with regard to their heterogeneity (see Figure 2.1). According to the U.S. Census Bureau, the AAPI racial category consists of 48 different ethnic groups that occupy positions along the full range of the socioeconomic

FIGURE 2.1 Key Indicators for the AAPI Community

Number of ethnicities	48
Number of languages spoken	300
Percent foreign born	69%
Percent below poverty	6% (Filipinos), 20% (Samoans), 38% (Hmong)

Note. From "The Relevance of Asian Americans & Pacific Islanders in the College Completion Agenda," p. 6, by the National Commission on Asian American and Pacific Islander Research in Education, 2011, www.nyu.edu/projects/care/docs/2011_CARE _Report.pdf. Copyright 2011 by the National Commission on Asian American and Pacific Islander Research in Education.

spectrum, from the poor and underprivileged to the affluent and highly skilled (U.S. Census Bureau, 2000). AAPIs also vary demographically with regard to language background, immigration history, culture, and religion (National Commission on Asian American Research in Education, 2008).

Consider that while a significant proportion of immigrants from Asia come to the United States already highly educated, others enter from countries that have provided only limited opportunities for educational and social mobility. Pacific Islanders, defined as people whose origins are from Polynesia, Micronesia, or Melanesia, are a diverse panethnic group whose national histories include the struggle for sovereignty. Yet, these and other very unique circumstances are often overshadowed by being grouped with the larger AAPI racial categorization. Thus, while the AAPI population represents a single entity in certain contexts such as for interracial group comparisons, it is equally important to understand that the demography of the population is made up of a complex set of social realities for the individuals and communities that fall in this category.

Therefore, in addition to negotiating forms of subordination enacted because of race, AAPIs in the United States are forced to straddle other intersecting identities as well: those of ethnicity and nationality, foreign status, and being first-generation immigrants or children of immigrants. Among Asian Americans, for example, Southeast Asians have a high incidence of refugee status and have experienced significant economic, political, cultural, and linguistic challenges that have an adverse impact on their education and social mobility. The inclusion of subgroups like Southeast Asians and Pacific Islanders in research and policy is also further challenged by inaccurate, incomplete, misleading, and often unreliable data that do not well represent the population relative to other groups (Teranishi, 2010).

An intersectional perspective on AAPIs is further complicated when we consider gender. Intersectionality has mainly been applied to Black women in the context of feminist thought. It has not been employed as an analytical tool for critically examining the relevance of social categories, and the boundaries between them, to understand how various forms of oppression have an impact on the lives of other minority groups, including AAPIs (Nash, 2008; Teranishi, 2002). This is particularly important given the impact on AAPIs of the forces of oppression related to ethnicity, immigration status, and the particular racialization of AAPI males, which are unique to each of the various AAPI communities (Teranishi, Behringer, Grey, & Parker, 2009). Thus, what follows is a discussion regarding the need for a more nuanced and intersectional perspective when considering the educational experiences and outcomes of AAPI males. Capturing the heterogeneity in the population not only creates a new discourse for AAPI males, it expands understanding of the issues that have an impact on minority males. This is particularly important for shedding light on the unique needs and challenges of AAPI male subgroups and for creating more inclusive policies for the most marginalized and vulnerable among these groups.

Ethnic and Gender Differences in Educational Attainment Among AAPIs

Data disaggregated by ethnicity and gender reveal a complicated portrait of educational mobility for the AAPI community. Using an intersectional perspective, this section looks at AAPIs' educational attainment among and between ethnic and gender groups. First, we examine secondary education outcomes. Second, we discuss the persistence and degree attainment rate among AAPI college students. Finally, we discuss how a deeper understanding of ethnicity and gender is revealed through an age-cohort analysis that captures differences in intergenerational educational mobility. While this section assesses differences in educational attainment among AAPI male subgroups, it does not offer a discussion about causation. Rather, it focuses on a descriptive portrait of conditions and outcomes that needs further examination relative to the role and function of race and gender in the AAPI community.

Educational Attainment at the Secondary Education Level

Data disaggregated by ethnicity and gender reveal significant differences between males from the various AAPI subgroups with regard to rates of high school dropout, completion, and college going among high school graduates (see Table 2.1). While East Asian (Chinese, Japanese, and Korean) and South Asian (Asian Indian, Bangladeshi, and Pakistani) males have over a 90 percent high school completion rate and less than a 10 percent dropout rate, Southeast Asian (Cambodian, Hmong, Laotian, and Vietnamese) and Pacific Islander (Guamanian, Samoan, and Tongan) males have a high school completion rate of around 85 percent and a dropout rate of around 15 percent (authors' calculations using data from U.S. Census Bureau, n.d.). Among these groups of male high school graduates, fewer are attending college.

The data reveal differences in the gaps between AAPI men and women with regard to high school completion and college-going outcomes. Some groups—Asian Indians, Chinese, Japanese, and Koreans—more or less exhibit parity between women and men with regard to high school completion and noncompletion and college-going rates among high school graduates. In some communities—Bangladeshi, Pakistani, and Cambodian—men experience better educational outcomes compared to women when it comes to high school

TABLE 2.1
Precollege Educational Attainment of 25- to 34-Year-Old AAPIs by Ethnicity and Gender, 2008–2010

	Did Not Complete High School		*High School Diploma or Equivalent*		*High School Graduates Attending College*	
	Male	*Female*	*Male*	*Female*	*Male*	*Female*
Asian Americans						
Asian Indian	2.5%	2.5%	97.5%	97.5%	94.7%	94.8%
Bangladeshi	8.8%	13.2%	91.2%	86.8%	81.9%	71.5%
Chinese	7.2%	6.5%	92.8%	93.5%	90.2%	91.4%
Filipino	3.9%	2.4%	96.1%	97.6%	83.1%	89.0%
Indonesian	1.4%	3.0%	98.6%	97.0%	84.8%	87.0%
Japanese	2.0%	1.9%	98.0%	98.1%	89.2%	90.7%
Korean	1.8%	1.4%	98.2%	98.6%	90.6%	92.0%
Malaysian	9.3%	8.2%	90.7%	91.8%	94.7%	93.4%
Pakistani	5.4%	8.9%	94.6%	91.1%	86.4%	79.4%
Sri Lankan	1.3%	0.0%	98.7%	100.0%	93.9%	89.7%
Thai	7.6%	7.2%	92.4%	92.8%	81.4%	85.8%
Cambodian	14.3%	17.3%	85.7%	82.7%	67.9%	63.6%
Hmong	14.7%	12.8%	85.3%	87.2%	64.8%	69.6%
Laotian	16.7%	13.1%	83.3%	86.9%	58.5%	71.3%
Vietnamese	11.4%	13.4%	88.6%	86.6%	82.5%	78.3%
Pacific Islanders						
Guamanian	15.7%	6.0%	84.3%	94.0%	65.4%	61.5%
Native Hawaiian	5.1%	6.0%	94.9%	94.0%	49.2%	69.0%
Samoan	12.7%	7.4%	87.3%	92.6%	46.8%	56.5%
Tongan	16.7%	13.5%	83.3%	86.5%	43.2%	55.6%

Note. From authors' calculations using data from "American Community Survey, 2006–2008, Three-Year Estimates [data]," by U.S. Census Bureau, n.d., http://factfinder2.census.gov.

completion and college going among high school graduates. However, for a number of AAPI ethnic subgroups, including Hmong, Laotians, Samoans, Tongans, and Guamanians, males are far less likely to complete high school or enroll in college if they do finish high school, compared to their female counterparts. The differences between males and females are as high as 10 percent in high school completion (for Guamanian males) and 20 percent for college going among high school graduates (for Native Hawaiians; authors' calculations using data from U.S. Census Bureau, n.d.). For some groups, such as Filipinos and Indonesians, men and woman have comparable high school completion rates, but male high school graduates are less likely to attend college.

Educational Attainment Among College Attendees

Looking at the gender differences in college completion patterns for each of the AAPI ethnic subgroups also reveals disparities at the tertiary level (see Table 2.2). Some groups of AAPI men—primarily East Asian and South

TABLE 2.2
Educational Attainment of 25- to 34-Year-Old AAPI College Attendees by Ethnicity and Gender, 2008–2010

	Some College, No Degree		Associate Degree Only		Bachelor's Degree or More	
	Male	*Female*	*Male*	*Female*	*Male*	*Female*
Asian Americans						
Asian Indian	6.2%	6.8%	2.7%	3.6%	91.1%	89.5%
Bangladeshi	18.7%	22.3%	6.5%	7.3%	74.8%	70.4%
Chinese	12.3%	10.6%	5.2%	6.4%	82.5%	83.0%
Filipino	33.4%	26.7%	16.9%	12.6%	49.7%	60.7%
Indonesian	20.9%	19.4%	11.2%	10.2%	68.0%	70.5%
Japanese	19.4%	15.3%	8.0%	13.5%	72.6%	71.2%
Korean	24.5%	17.7%	6.1%	7.6%	69.4%	74.7%
Malaysian	6.8%	7.1%	9.5%	5.4%	83.7%	87.4%
Pakistani	17.2%	18.1%	5.6%	9.0%	77.2%	72.8%
Sri Lankan	21.8%	12.4%	3.1%	7.4%	75.1%	80.1%

(Continues)

TABLE 2.2 (Continued)

	Some College, No Degree		Associate Degree Only		Bachelor's Degree or More	
	Male	*Female*	*Male*	*Female*	*Male*	*Female*
Thai	20.6%	14.2%	13.4%	6.0%	66.0%	79.8%
Cambodian	45.9%	50.8%	20.3%	11.6%	33.8%	37.6%
Hmong	56.9%	46.5%	16.8%	20.7%	26.4%	32.7%
Laotian	52.3%	47.7%	16.2%	15.2%	31.5%	37.1%
Vietnamese	32.3%	28.1%	11.5%	10.6%	56.2%	61.3%
Pacific Islanders						
Guamanian	55.5%	53.4%	17.5%	14.5%	27.0%	32.1%
Native Hawaiian	56.4%	56.7%	12.1%	19.0%	31.5%	24.4%
Samoan	61.6%	64.5%	18.7%	11.6%	19.7%	23.9%
Tongan	44.7%	54.8%	24.5%	12.9%	30.9%	32.3%

Note. From authors' calculations using data from "American Community Survey, 2006–2008, Three-Year Estimates [data]," by U.S. Census Bureau, n.d., http://factfinder2.census.gov.

Asian—have a lower likelihood of dropping out of college and a higher likelihood of obtaining a bachelor's degree or more as their highest level of education compared to men from other AAPI subgroups. In fact, the gaps between men from the various subgroups are very striking. For example, among Southeast Asians and Pacific Islanders, one-third to two-thirds of the men leave college without earning a degree, compared to less than one-fifth of the men from East and South Asian backgrounds (authors' calculations using data from U.S. Census Bureau, n.d.). Southeast Asian and Pacific Islander men are also far more likely to obtain an associate's degree as their highest level of education compared to East and South Asian men.

In most cases, AAPI males are more likely than their female counterparts to drop out of college. In some cases, the gaps between men and women are quite pronounced. For example, twice as many Cambodian and Tongan males who attended college earned an associate's degree as their highest level of education compared to their female counterparts, who were more likely to earn baccalaureate degrees. Gaps in completing a bachelor's degree or higher among college attendees is at least 10 percentage points for Filipino and Thai males compared to their female counterparts. In fact, for all AAPI subgroups in which completing at least a bachelor's degree is already low, as it is for

Laotians, Cambodians, Hmong, Guamanians, Samoans, and Tongans, the outcomes of males trail those of females.

Intergenerational Educational Mobility

The story of educational mobility for AAPIs is even more complicated, with some ethnic subgroups experiencing rising rates of educational attainment while other subgroups are declining. Moreover, in some ethnic subgroups men and women are experiencing upward intergenerational educational mobility, while among other groups there are significant differences between men and women in the direction of their mobility. This section untangles intergenerational educational mobility between ethnic subgroups with attention to gender differences.

While policymakers would like to see a higher rate of educational attainment among younger cohorts of students, the educational attainment rates of 55- to 64-year-olds compared to 25- to 34-year-olds in the nation overall only show a modest increase in baccalaureate attainment. For example, we see that the rate of bachelor's degree attainment for the U.S. population age 25–34 (34 percent) was only four percentage points higher than it was for the 55- to 64-year-old cohort (30 percent; authors' calculations using data from U.S. Census Bureau, 2008–2010). However, these data conceal important trends along gender lines when examining intergenerational data. In particular, in the U.S. population, regardless of race, younger cohorts of women (35 percent of 25- to 34-year-olds) have been experiencing upward intergenerational educational mobility compared to older cohorts of women (27 percent of 55- to 64-year-olds). On the other hand, outcomes for young men (27 percent of 25- to 24-year-olds) have been declining compared to older cohorts of men (32 percent of 55- to 64-year-olds; authors' calculations using data from U.S. Census Bureau, 2008–2010).

For males of color, some trends in intergenerational educational attainment are a problem on two levels when it comes to intergenerational mobility. First, there is a significantly lower rate of educational attainment among older cohorts of males of color relative to older cohorts of White men. This is indicative of limited access to educational opportunities for males of color in the 1960s and 1970s. Second, the gaps between minority men and White men are actually increasing rather than decreasing, which has further accentuated the divide between men along racial lines. These two disturbing trends of downward intergenerational educational mobility are evident when viewing the bachelor's degree attainment rate of Black men. While 18 percent of 55- to 64-year-old Black men have a bachelor's degree or more, only 15 percent of 25- to 34-year-old Black men do. Thus, while the gap in bachelor's degree attainment between 55- to 64-year-old Black men and all men in that age cohort was 12 percent, it has increased to 19 percent among 25- to 34-year-old Black men relative to the younger cohort of all men (authors' calculations using data from U.S. Census Bureau, 2008–2010).

While downward intergenerational mobility among Black men has caught the attention of educators, policymakers, and the mainstream public (e.g., Acs, 2011; Kearney, 2006), intergenerational mobility among AAPI men has not received any attention. Yet, looking at the college-going rates of high school graduates across AAPI ethnic groups, we find a number of instances where the younger cohort of women increased their access to college, while men showed declines. This is the case among Guamanians where almost 59 percent of men aged 55 to 64 years attended college, compared to about 55 percent of men aged 25 to 34 years (see Figure 2.2). However, women made gains in college participation from the older generation to the younger one. While almost 54 percent of Guamanian women 55 to 64 years of age attended college, it increased to almost 58 percent among 25- to 34-year-olds (authors' calculations using data from U.S. Census Bureau, 2008–2010). Figure 2.3 represents the college participation rate of Native Hawaiians by age cohort and gender. Similar to Guamanians, the older cohort of Native Hawaiian men (55 to 64) had a higher college-going rate than the younger cohort of men, while the younger age cohort of women had a higher college-going rate than the older cohort of women. These data demonstrate that even at the level of ethnicity, gender differences in college participation can be concealed by not considering AAPI men and women

FIGURE 2.2 College-Going Rates Among Guamanians by Gender and Age Cohort, 2008–2010

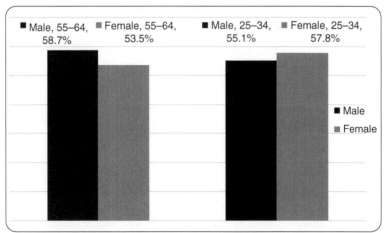

Note. From authors' calculations using data from "American Community Survey, 2006–2008, Three-Year Estimates [data]," by U.S. Census Bureau, n.d., http://factfinder2.census.gov.

FIGURE 2.3 College-Going Rates Among Native Hawaiians by Gender and Age Cohort, 2008–2010

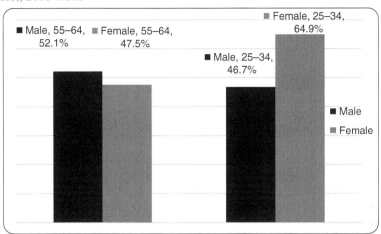

Note. From authors' calculations using data from "American Community Survey, 2006–2008, Three-Year Estimates [data]," by U.S. Census Bureau, n.d., http://factfinder2.census.gov.

separately. More specific to the intergenerational education attainment of Guamanians and Native Hawaiians, declines in the college participation rates of men are concealed by significant gains by women.

Differences also exist in degree attainment rates by ethnicity and gender among a subset of college attendees. Among Filipinos, for example, the bachelor's degree attainment rate among college students is lower for men 25 to 34 years of age than it is for men 55 to 64 years of age. However, Filipino women 25 to 34 years of age show a higher bachelor's degree attainment rate than women aged 55 to 64 (authors' calculations using data from U.S. Census Bureau, 2008–2010). What happened to Filipino men who attended college? The younger cohort of Filipino men was 75 percent more likely than their older counterparts to have an associate's degree as their highest level of education. These trends are displayed in Figure 2.4. Similar trends in bachelor's degree attainment for Korean men and women are occurring, as seen in Figure 2.5, where Korean men show a decline in the younger age cohort compared to the older one, while younger Korean women are experiencing higher rates of college completion with a bachelor's degree or more. While young Filipino men who attended college showed a higher rate of earning an associate degree compared to their older counterparts, younger Korean men were 32 percent more likely than their older counterparts to leave college with no degree (authors' calculations using data from U.S. Census Bureau, 2008–2010).

Differences by age cohorts among other ethnic groups are also evident. We see upward social mobility in the Thai, Vietnamese, and Tongan

FIGURE 2.4 B.A. Attainment Among Filipino College Attendees by Gender and Age Cohort, 2008–2010

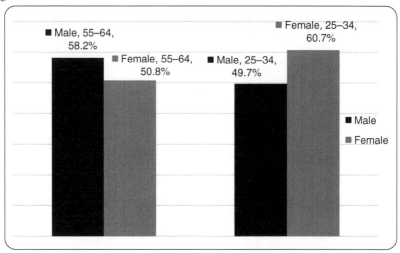

Note. From authors' calculations using data from "American Community Survey, 2006–2008, Three-Year Estimates [data]," by U.S. Census Bureau, n.d., http://factfinder2.census.gov.

FIGURE 2.5 B.A. Attainment Among Korean College Attendees by Gender and Age Cohort, 2008–2010

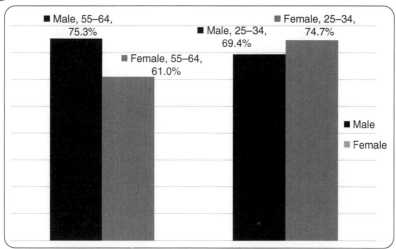

Note. From authors' calculations using data from "American Community Survey, 2006–2008, Three-Year Estimates [data]," by U.S. Census Bureau, n.d., http://factfinder2.census.gov.

communities, but the trend is much more marked for women than it is for men. For instance, among the Thai population, not only do women exhibit higher rates of baccalaureate attainment, but the gains made by young women are more than four times greater than the gains made by men over time. Among the Vietnamese and Tongans, the share of younger people with a bachelor's degree or higher is greater than the share of those who are older, but the gains made by young women exceed the gains made by young men by 8 to 10 percentage points (authors' calculations using data from U.S. Census Bureau, 2008–2010).

These trends of downward educational mobility among men are very alarming and point to the need for a more concerted effort to better represent these populations in discourse on the needs and challenges of minority men. Action in this area is especially urgent given that for some AAPI subgroups, gender gaps in college participation and degree attainment rates are widening instead of narrowing.

From a Theoretical Frame to Mobilization and Action

The model minority myth is perhaps the single most damaging issue for the AAPI community. It affects how AAPIs are perceived and treated by others because oversimplified generalizations prevent people from acknowledging the complexities faced by individuals or subgroups within the population. The stereotype has led to racism, prejudice, and discrimination on the interpersonal and structural levels. Finally, it affects how AAPIs as individuals and as a group view themselves. Stacey Lee (2009), author of *Unraveling the "Model Minority" Stereotype: Listening to Asian American Youth"*, found that AAPI students internalize the myth and assess themselves according to this image, which is a problem because the image of the model minority is often unattainable in reality.

In 2004 Jack Tchen and Robert Teranishi at New York University developed the National Commission on Asian American and Pacific Islander research in Education (CARE), which received initial funding and support from the College Board. This effort was in response to a pressing need for more and better research to help transcend the model minority myth. Since its inception, CARE has produced a number of research reports, policy briefs, and academic articles that have armed policymakers, advocacy groups, and practitioners with research and data on the conditions and outcomes of AAPIs in higher education.

One of CARE's strengths, beyond offering empirical perspectives on the population, has been in its conceptual approach to thinking about the AAPI population. CARE administrators believe that for any marginalized population, using stereotypes as the basis for practice or policy will not lead to a better understanding of the problem and cannot lead to any viable solutions. Research that is driven by narrow understandings of race only perpetuates the use of stereotypes and generalizations. CARE officials also believe that the work should not be reactionary in its approach to research, practice, and policy. It must be based on alternative perspectives that demonstrate how research can transcend the conceptual blockages that have severely limited the knowledge that exists about AAPIs, their education, and their social mobility in America. Moving toward practice and policy that places value on those who are on the periphery requires research that can address the unique demography of AAPIs and how it is characteristically similar to, or unique in regard to, other populations in America.

In addition to reconceptualized research, CARE officials believe that research, practice, and policy making should not occur in a vacuum, and that research should be a collaborative process that directly engages communities, institutions, and the policy arena. This process brings to the table divergent vantage points and constituents with different types of experience and expertise. A collaborative research model creates a process of inquiry that enables colleagues in and outside university settings to collectively determine how to frame problems and how to address them empirically. This collaborative model is imperative at all stages of the research process, including setting goals, identifying and understanding problems that inhibit goals, and creating solutions to address them. For example, CARE has produced a number of reports (e.g., National Commission on Asian American Research in Education, 2008), with College Board support, demonstrating why disaggregated data for AAPIs is crucial for understanding their educational trajectories and identifying ways subgroups are being underserved even as they are popularly understood as having experienced unalloyed success. These reports highlight the intersectional approach, examining how the confluence of race, ethnicity, immigration status, and gender influences educational outcomes for AAPIs. Based on this research, CARE has formed partnerships with stakeholders and policymakers at Educational Testing Service (ETS) and the U.S. Department of Education to consider ways they can put findings from research into practice to improve data collection and policy making that is sensitive to the needs of AAPI subgroups. As part of this effort, CARE is verifying the extent to which disaggregated data are currently collected by federal agencies for AAPIs, examining potential models for disaggregated data collection from the state or postsecondary system levels, and trying to discover any administrative or other issues that impede consistent and timely disaggregated data collection for AAPIs at the national level.

CARE has also extended its intersectional research-to-practice approach with minority-serving institutions. Most recently, CARE has been collaborating with campus-based professionals to study how Asian American and Native American Pacific Islander–Serving Institutions (AANAPISIs) can enhance success for their AAPI populations. AANAPISIs represent the newest federal designation for minority-serving institutions eligible to apply for federal funding for capacity-building purposes. The first cohort of institutions received funding through this program in 2008. In partnership with colleagues from three AANAPISI-designated community colleges, CARE has developed a slate of inquiry activities to engage professionals at each campus and gain insights into which unique AAPI subgroups are represented and the extent to which they are being served. The inquiry activities have taken a variety of forms to accommodate the major concerns and initiatives of each setting. For instance, civic engagement is a central part of the identity of one campus, which is examining ways its AAPI students and their home communities are (or are not) involved in these initiatives, and the influence such initiatives have on strengthening their academic success and leadership development. It is also focusing on the extent to which Filipino students have been represented in these initiatives and the extent to which these students' outcomes show educational inequities. Another partner college is examining the impact of its efforts to attract and engage Pacific Islander students. This institution is located in a neighborhood with a significant Pacific Islander diaspora, but its youth, particularly males, have historically not felt welcome at this campus and have chosen not to attend. The college has been assessing its engagement efforts and is trying new strategies. For example, it recently hosted a conference for 300 Pacific Islander high school students and their families to provide information about college going (R. Fonoti, personal communication, October 31, 2012).

CARE is attempting to connect theory, research, and action. The experience of working with the AANAPISI campuses has highlighted the power of working collaboratively with other stakeholders. CARE is now supporting efforts to help AANAPISIs create an umbrella organization known as the Asian Pacific Islander Association of Colleges and Universities (APIACU) to facilitate more collaboration among the campuses in sharing best practices for serving AAPI students, to assist in connecting to community-based organizations as an additional source of support for students and their home communities, and working with policymakers to secure additional resources. Forums such as APIACU provide an opportunity to deepen the conversation with a variety of stakeholders—institutional leaders, community organizations, and policymakers—about ways to better serve AAPI students by calling attention not only to subgroup differences but to differences by gender.

Conclusion

Positioning AAPI males as part of America's equity agenda requires transcending the intellectual boundaries that have severely limited—and even undermined—our knowledge about their educational opportunities and outcomes. In many cases, studies are not designed to critically acknowledge, examine, or appreciate the heterogeneity that exists among AAPIs generally and the complexity presented by adding gender to the analysis. Rather, comparative racial frameworks assume that the AAPI racial category as a whole—with regard to race and gender—is consistently homogeneous and equally comparable to other racial groups. As a result, the actual educational experiences and processes of AAPI students in the aggregate, and as distinct parts, are often concealed.

A perspective of intersectionality reveals how existing research paradigms that are commonly applied to the study of race and gender neither promote a better understanding about any individual racial or gender group nor provide a perspective that allows us to constructively improve the educational experiences or outcomes of subgroups. A particular problem is that race and gender, singularly and intersectionally, are complex social phenomena that are difficult to define and conceptualize. We demonstrate that the dominant Black/White paradigm cannot provide the nuanced perspective needed to understand the educational mobility of AAPI students, particularly when it comes to gender differences in the population. This is particularly true among the most marginalized and vulnerable populations of AAPI men—Pacific Islanders and Southeast Asians—whose educational attainment departs the most from AAPIs in the aggregate.

Finally, this chapter points to the need to understand the dynamic nature of race and ethnicity in America, which is particularly relevant as the nation continues to change significantly with regard to its demography. An intersectional perspective on the educational mobility of AAPI males demonstrates why this point is important for social policy, research, and educational practice. And, while we point to AAPI men in this chapter, this is also an important perspective to consider for other minority male subgroups. It is through a more nuanced perspective that we can gain a better understanding of and construct a more appropriate response to the inequitable educational conditions and outcomes being found among minority males.

Note

1. See books by Helen Zia and others who have written about Vincent Chin, Wen Ho Lee, and other AAPIs who have faced incidents of racism and xenophobia.

References

Acs, G. (2011). *Downward mobility from the middle class: Waking up from the American dream*. Washington, DC: Pew Charitable Trusts. Retrieved October 1, 2012, from http://www.pewtrusts.org/uploadedFiles/wwwpewtrustsorg/Reports/Economic _Mobility/Pew_PollProject_Final_SP.pdf

Bell, D. (1987). *And we are not saved: The elusive quest for racial justice*. New York, NY: Basic Books.

Brand, D. (1987, August 31). Education: The new whiz kids. *Time*. Retrieved October 1, 2012, from http://www.time.com/time/magazine/article/0,9171,965326,00.html

Chang, M. J., Witt-Sandis, D., & Hakuta, K. (1999). The dynamics of race in higher education: An examination of the evidence. *Equity & Excellence in Education, 32*(2), 12–16.

Crenshaw, K. (1989). *Demarginalizing the intersection of race and sex: A Black feminist critique of antidiscrimination doctrine, feminist theory, and antiracist politics*. Paper presented at the meeting of the University of Chicago Legal Forum, Chicago, IL.

Crenshaw, K. (1991). Mapping the margins: Intersectionality, identity politics, and violence against women of color. *Stanford Law Review, 43*(6), 1241–1299.

Delgado, R., & Stefanic, J. (2012). *Critical race theory: An introduction* (2nd ed.). New York, NY: NYU Press.

Kearney, M. S. (2006). Intergenerational mobility for women and minorities in the United States. *The Future of Children, 16*(2), 37–53.

Kristof, N. D. (2006, May 14). The model students. *The New York Times*, p. WK13.

Lee, S. J. (2009). *Unraveling the "Model Minority" Stereotype: Listening to Asian American Youth*. New York: Teachers College.

Lee, S. J., & Kumashiro, K. K. (2005). *A report on the status of Asian Americans and Pacific Islanders in education: Beyond the "model minority" stereotype*. Washington, DC: National Educational Association.

Lee, W. H., & Zia, H. (2002). *My country versus me: The first-hand account by the Los Alamos scientist who was falsely accused of being a spy*. New York, NY: Hyperion.

Lei, J. L. (2003). (Un)necessary toughness? Those "loud Black girls" and those "quiet Asian boys." *Anthropology & Education Quarterly, 34*(2), 158–181.

Nash, J. C. (2008). Re-thinking intersectionality. *Feminist Review, 89*, 1–15.

National Commission on Asian American and Pacific Islander Research in Education. (2011). *The relevance of Asian Americans & Pacific Islanders in the college completion agenda*. Retrieved October 1, 2012, from http://www.nyu.edu/ projects/care/docs/2011_CARE_Report.pdf

National Commission on Asian American Research in Education. (2008). *Asian Americans and Pacific Islanders: Facts, not fiction: Setting the record straight*. Retrieved October 1, 2012, from http://www.nyu.edu/projects/care/docs/2008 _CARE_Report.pdf

Petersen, W. (1966, January 9). Success story, Japanese-American style. *The New York Times*, 20–21, 33, 36, 38, 40–41, 43.

Pew Research Center. (2012). *The rise of Asian Americans*. Retrieved October 1, 2012, from http://www.pewsocialtrends.org/2012/06/19/the-rise-of-asian-americans/

Success story of one minority group in U.S. (1966, December 26). *U.S. News & World Report.* Retrieved October 1, 2012, from http://www.dartmouth.edu/~hist32/Hist33/US%20News%20&%20World%20Report.pdf

Success story: Outwhiting the Whites. (1971, June 21). *Newsweek*, p. 24.

Teranishi, R. T. (2002). The myth of the super minority: Misconceptions about Asian Americans. *College Board Review, 195*, 16–21.

Teranishi, R. T. (2010). *Asians in the ivory tower: Dilemmas of racial inequality in American higher education.* New York, NY: Teachers College Press.

Teranishi, R. T., Behringer, L. B., Grey, E. A., & Parker, T. L. (2009). Critical race theory and research on Asian Americans and Pacific Islanders in higher education. *New Directions for Institutional Research: Conducting Research on Asian Americans in Higher Education*, no. 142, 57–68. doi:10.1002/ir.296

U.S. Census Bureau. (2000). *Summary file 1.* Retrieved November 11, 2013, from http://www.census.gov/census2000/sumfile1.html

U.S. Census Bureau. (2008–2010). *American Community Survey Public Use Microdata Sample, 2008–2010, three-year estimates* [data]. Retrieved October 1, 2012, from http://factfinder2.census.gov

U.S. Census Bureau. (n.d.). *American Community Survey, 2006–2008, three-year estimates* [data]. Retrieved October 1, 2012, from http://factfinder2.census.gov

3

AHISTORICISM IN THE NATIVE AMERICAN EXPERIENCE

LeManuel Lee Bitsói and Lloyd L. Lee

I felt invisible [in college] but mostly because I made myself invisible. I didn't feel in place and I always felt like I was different or not quite the same as everyone.
(L. L. Bitsói, personal communication, November 11, 2012)

Historical challenges and barriers have forced Native Americans into an ahistorical existence based on their intersectionality and invisibility, and many people are not aware of such inhibiting factors.[1] Hence, a majority of Americans do not understand why Native Americans cannot *just* go to school, *just* graduate from high school, then *just* go to college and *just* graduate with a bachelor's degree. Why is it so difficult to do *just* that, like other Americans? Much of the federal policy that has shaped education also shaped health care policy for American Indian people, and many in America today are not aware of the federal treaties that were made to guarantee education and health care for indigenous people in the United States. Today, some people question the relevance of this trust responsibility to the First Americans of this country: Why doesn't everyone receive free health care and education? To answer this question, we must first understand Native American history, for it is not always taught or acknowledged in American classrooms. The important role Native Americans played in the nation building of America is often relegated to minimal paragraphs and footnotes; therefore, American history needs to be understood through an indigenous lens. As the number of Native researchers, scientists, and educators has increased, they have begun to make inroads in deciphering how education, research (using various forms of critical race theory [CRT]), and health care can be controlled and conducted by American Indians and their tribal nations. This empowerment is what Sisseton Wahpeton Oyate Dakota scholar Kimberly TallBear (2013) has titled *democratizing science* (and technology).

We begin this chapter with an overview of what American Indian people have endured to thrive as miracle survivors despite the colonialism, imperialism, patriarchy, and genocide that began in 1492. Next, we discuss ahistoricism and misportrayals of Native Americans in view of the lack of awareness of indigenous history that has led to a profound misunderstanding of indigenous peoples. Then, we shed light on invisibility issues that stem from historical barriers that contribute to contemporary challenges American Indians and Alaska Natives face in higher education. (This information is necessary to comprehend how Native Americans have navigated education in this country. A historical context is provided, along with various societal constructs that have shaped their collective experience.) We then shift toward the contemporary experience by presenting snapshots of enrollment and graduation rates to illustrate how Native Americans compare with, and lag behind, other racial/ethnic groups in the United States (These figures also show that colleges and universities are doing a better job educating and graduating foreign students than indigenous people of North America.) As other contributors in this volume have used CRT to illustrate their positionality in this educational crisis, we introduce Tribal CRT (TribalCrit) and Native feminism as well as intersectionality to address the educational challenges of Native Americans. According to Brayboy (2006), "TribalCrit emerged from CRT and is rooted in the multiple, nuanced, and historically- and geographically-located epistemologies and ontologies found in Indigenous communities" (p. 427). In addition, we discuss the importance of traditional perspectives and roles (in the contemporary context) to demonstrate that success for Native Americans is not always a college degree. In addition to TribalCrit, the work of Native feminist scholars is presented to illustrate the importance of this emerging field and its impact on Native American men and accepted notions of heteronormative patriarchy. This provides a segue into our conclusion of plausible ways to address the various challenges Native Americans, especially males, face in graduating with an undergraduate degree. Our aim is to encourage a robust discussion and analysis that should be helpful to researchers, policymakers, and professionals, and assist in recruiting, retaining, and graduating an increased number of Native American men in higher education institutions.

A Nation of Nations

It is imperative to provide historical and general knowledge about American Indians and Alaska Natives to understand the Native American experience. First, the diversity among Native Americans is largely unknown to non-Natives, and this diversity makes tribal affiliation a more accurate approach for self-identification. Second, it is not common knowledge that tribal nations maintain their own customs, languages, traditions, and land bases (reservations).[2] Third, tribal nations are sovereign nations based on government-to-government relationships that are maintained with the federal government.[3] To that end, the federal government recognizes 566 Indian tribal nations in the United States, not including the 70 tribal nations recognized by state governments (Bureau of Indian Affairs, 2012). The National Congress of American Indians (2013) further describes the diversity of tribal nations by stating, "Two hundred and twenty-nine of these tribal nations are located in Alaska; the remaining tribes are located in 34 other states. In total, tribal governments exercise jurisdiction over lands that would make Indian Country the fourth largest state in the nation."

All tribal nations also determine their own requirements for citizenship and assign enrollment numbers (akin to federal Social Security numbers) that allow enrolled tribal citizens to receive any type of benefits—housing, medical care, scholarships, and revenue sharing. Tribal governments may have a president, chairman, or governor with councils or assemblies. This type of foreign governance evolved from federal governmental policies that were imposed to deculturalize indigenous people.[4]

Accepting foreign types of governance was inevitable, so civil rights activism (i.e., the American Indian Movement[5]) and federal legislation abolished policies instituted during the 19th and 20th centuries. As Native Americans continue to advance in self-governance, and as they stress the importance of treaty rights, some in society believe that historical issues are no longer relevant; however, remaining vestiges of colonialism and imperialism continue to influence society as well as educational opportunities for American Indians. Mishuana Goeman (2011) uses the term *settler colonialism* to describe such influence, because it "connotes the ongoing condition of settler occupation of Native land, an occupation so often pictured, monumentalized, and enforced by the containment of Native bodies and glorification of a colonial past" (p. 4). Also, research on indigenous people has determined that oppression and dominance still affect the developmental process for racial or ethnic identity (Evans, Forney, & Guido-DiBrito, 1998).

Given such negative conditions, it should not be surprising that the initial experience of American Indians and Alaska Natives with non-Native education was not congruent. Less than stellar experiences are also the result of the value systems and cultures indigenous people traditionally maintained that value cooperation over competition. Therefore, historical and invisibility issues become even more relevant in understanding the experience of American Indian students.

Native American Education

As previously stated, the roots of American Indian education stem from the colleges that were first established in the United States and the nine schools established in the colonial period: Harvard College, William and Mary, Dartmouth, Yale, University of Pennsylvania, Princeton, Columbia, Brown, and Rutgers. Of these nine colleges, three specifically focused on the education of indigenous peoples: Harvard College, William and Mary, and Dartmouth (Carney, 1999). Despite such written commitments to American Indian education, only five Indians enrolled at Harvard, and only one graduated between 1650 and 1693—the years the school's Indian College existed. The record for William and Mary's Indian College is not much better, as only 16 Indian students attended between 1723 and 1743, and none of them graduated.[6] Dartmouth had a better record than Harvard and William and Mary, as 25 Indian students enrolled and 3 graduated before 1800 (Belgarde, 1996; McClellan, Fox, & Lowe, 2005). Essentially, these three institutions included a commitment to American Indians in their charters only to secure funds from prospective donors in England, not for any noble purposes. Furthermore, Wright (1988) asserts that colonial college presidents "capitalized on Christian philanthropy [in England] to enhance the growth of their floundering and financially strapped colleges" (p. 12).

Treaty Obligations

After the colonial colleges failed to educate them, Native Americans sought to gain higher educational opportunities through treaty arrangements with the federal government. Between 1778 and 1871, 97 treaties addressing education for American Indians were signed by tribal nations and the federal government (Belgarde, 1996; McClellan et al., 2005), but almost none of those treaties was honored. The first treaty to provide any financial commitment for higher education for American Indians came in 1830, when the federal government signed a treaty with the Choctaw Nation stating that the government would provide funding for Choctaw citizens who pursued higher education (McLellan et al., 2005; Olivas, 1996). Beyond this federal commitment, very little else was done for Native American higher education. While there were many developments in higher education for African Americans and women during this time, there were none for American Indians (McClellan et al., 2005). The lack of federal support continued in spite of the Meriam Report of 1928, a study conducted by the federal government that provided recommendations for American Indian education.[7]

The passage of the Indian Reorganization Act of 1934 (Indian Reorganization Act, 1934/2013) was instrumental in acknowledging American Indian sovereignty and self-determination for tribal nations. However, along with this legislation, the federal government attempted to terminate all its obligations to Native Americans and to shift its treaty and trust responsibilities to state governments in the 1940s and 1950s. At this time, many American Indians were being forced to attend government boarding schools and trade schools hundreds of miles away from their homelands; it was the beginning of forced assimilation and the attempted destruction of American Indian culture. Needless to say, this federal policy was disastrous for Native Americans (Boyer, 1997). Families were uprooted and torn apart by this policy, and there was an unfortunate loss of Native languages and cultures.

In the 1960s the federal government reevaluated its termination policy and began to pursue self-determination policies instead. To empower tribal governments and communities, Native leaders began to focus on self-empowerment through the control of education during the civil rights movement. Daniel Wildcat (2001) asserted, "Democracy suggests people have a right to educate children in accordance with their societal values and beliefs," and questioned, "Why should we expect less in our Native communities?" (p. 139). Such efforts in education have advanced tribally controlled schools (and colleges) that promote Indian traditions and history.

Tribally Controlled Education

In addition to vastly improved federal policies governing tribal schools through the Bureau of Indian Education, tribal colleges and universities (TCUs) have been established. TCUs share a common mission to promote the culture of tribes and strengthen the economic and social status of a tribal community (Belgarde, 1996). Moreover, Guardia and Evans (2008) acknowledge that TCUs also work toward preserving tribal languages and cultures. This preservation led to the establishment of the first tribally controlled college in the United States—Navajo Community College—now known as Diné College (2012), which was established in 1968 in the Navajo Nation. According to the American Indian Higher Education Consortium (AIHEC, 2012), established in 1972 to assist the advancement of TCUs, there are currently 36 TCUs in the United States.

Today these colleges provide educational opportunities for students to pursue careers beyond their communities (Belgarde, 1996). American Indian students also enhance their personal and academic development through Native culture and language, instruction from indigenous faculty, and culturally appropriate support systems (Guardia & Evans, 2008). Furthermore, TCUs have contributed to the development of Native American Studies (NAS) in higher education and have inspired the development of over 130 NAS programs in colleges and universities throughout North America (Nelson, 2012).

Ahistoricism and Misportrayals

> *The image of the "Indian" is invented and does not exist within tribal communities, but has been produced by Whites in the dominant society to fulfill their need to create and own a "real Indian" they can control and manipulate.*
> (Brayboy & Searle, 2007, p. 177)

Historically, colleges and universities invented images of American Indians and used them as mascots to *honor* Native Americans. Incidentally, this usage can be traced to one of the colonial colleges.[8] This comes as no surprise since higher education in the United States is, as a whole, a White male institution that is paternalistic, patriarchal, hegemonic, and heteronormative. While the first colleges (namely, Harvard, Dartmouth, and William and Mary[9]) in North America were established to include the enrollment of indigenous people (under the guise of education, their aim was to Christianize infidels), they were really established by White men for White men. Wright (1988) confirms this by stating that colonists, "eager to maintain British sanction of their struggling settlements and institutions, capitalized on the religious fervor of the English, but for the most part neglected to fulfill their professed pious mission" (p. 2). Thus, anyone who has attended college in the United States has been conditioned and trained to think like White men. This has been the root of patriarchal, heteronormative, and racist notions in almost all aspects of higher education and society that still exist today. The exception could be minority-serving institutions (MSIs); however, they are still somewhat patterned after White mainstream institutions. Still, students who attend MSIs will receive a more culturally sensitive and appropriate higher education that is tangible and relevant to their worldviews and lives. This is especially true for TCUs, for their primary mission is to preserve indigenous languages and cultures that value cooperation over competition as opposed to the competitive ethos of White heteronormative America.

While one can compile a litany of atrocities that Native Americans have experienced, we intentionally highlight two examples of (in)visibility and paternalism in our nation's history. For a moment, imagine yourself featured as a sideshow for a circus because you looked like a "real" Indian. Now imagine what Tatonka-I-Yatanka (Sitting Bull) felt when he was being paraded around as part of Buffalo Bill's Wild West Show. Sitting Bull was a Hunkpapa Lakota Sioux chief and holy man who led his people to resist the U.S. government's efforts to exterminate them. As a leader of the Sioux, Sitting Bull led his defense force of protectors to a major victory at the Battle of the Little Bighorn against Lt. Col. George Armstrong Custer and the 7th Cavalry on June 25, 1876 ("Sitting Bull," 2013). Soon thereafter, Sitting Bull was a wanted man, so he fled with some of his people to Canada. He eventually returned to U.S. territories and surrendered to U.S. troops on July 19, 1881. He was recruited to join the Wild West Show, but after a year he returned to live among his people ("New Perspectives on the

West: William F. Cody," 2001). Upon his return, he was still considered to be a threat, and, although he was unarmed, he was killed while being placed under house arrest on December 15, 1890 ("Sitting Bull," 2013).

In addition, there is an ongoing lack of respect or recognition of American Indians as people. This is clearly evident in "Operation Geronimo," now infamously known as the code used in the U.S. military mission to kill Osama bin Laden (Mazzetti, Cooper, & Baker, 2011). This code name was confirmed in the book *No Easy Day* by former U.S. Navy SEAL Mark Owen (real name Matt Bissonnette), who participated in the mission (Owen & Maurer, 2012). For the record, Geronimo, or Goyathley, was the leader of the Chiricahua Apache who defied the U.S. government and eluded capture for years. His military genius was astounding; the U.S. government reportedly used 5,000 soldiers and 500 volunteers along with 3,000 Mexicans to capture him (Brayboy & Searle, 2007). When he finally turned himself in, he was sentenced to two years with the promise that he would be able to return to his homeland, but he soon became a prisoner of war and died in 1909 at Fort Sill, Oklahoma, of complications from pneumonia. Needless to say, the naming of the mission, however random or unintentional, perpetuates negative stereotypes of Native Americans. Goyathley and Tatonka-I-Yatanka are heroes to Native Americans (and the American spirit), and they should be remembered as such. Thus, an overall theme of this chapter is to inform society that Native Americans are not the stereotypical representations non-Native people expect them to be— romanticized figures from the past stored in museums to be viewed as curios.[10]

(In)visibility

Like the Asian American and Pacific Islander population, Native Americans are often misunderstood and miscategorized. The portrayal of American Indian people in the United States is often inaccurate and incomplete in society and education. It is as if Native Americans never existed in the Americas. In Journell's (2009) study of the representation of indigenous people in social studies courses in this country, he found that American Indians and Alaska Natives continue to be misportrayed in American public education. In addition to other researchers (Banks, 1993; Ladson-Billings, 2003), Journell also asserts that American history taught in public schools "caters to a Eurocentric male point of view, starting with the voyage of Columbus and continuing with English colonization over a century later" (p. 19), which is drenched in patriarchy and paternalism.

Thus, one can deduce that these misrepresentations and misportrayals from hegemonic and heteronormative perspectives contribute to present-day Native American invisibility. Moreover, Brayboy and Searle (2007) state, "The invisibility of American Indians is intimately connected to the ways they have been made visible by the government, in schools, and within popular media" (p. 173). Inevitably, the invisibility of Native Americans seeps into higher education (Brayboy, 2004). In an attempt to ameliorate invisibility, Brayboy and Searle also ingeniously use the term *(in)visible* to describe a "mutually-constituted relation" where "visibility and invisibility constantly exist as two sides of the same coin" (p. 174).

Contemporary Issues

According to the report *Higher Education: Gaps in Access and Persistence Study* (Ross et al., 2012),

> Among 9th-grade students in 2009, a lower percentage of males than females (53 vs. 59 percent) expected to complete a bachelor's or graduate/ professional degree as their highest level of education. Conversely, a higher percentage of males than females (17 vs. 12 percent) expected their highest level of education to be the completion of high school or less. (p. 134)

Furthermore,

> 60 percent of Asian males, 59 percent of males of two or more races, 56 percent of White males, and 54 percent of Black males expected to complete at least a bachelor's degree, compared with 44 percent of Hispanic males and 33 percent of American Indian/Alaska Native males. (Ross et al., 2012, p. 134)

Thus, it can be deduced that because of a variety of challenging factors, American Indian/Alaska Native males already do not expect to graduate from college or even high school, as shown in Table 3.1.

Contemporary Challenges

While Native Americans face many barriers and challenges, arguably, the two most notable are those described by Pewewardy and Frey (2004), who reiterate McDonald's (1992) observation that "American Indian college students are often cited as the most underrepresented of minority students attending post-secondary educational institutions" (p. 34), and Suina's (1987) assertion that American Indians "are the most underserved and least noticed ethnic group in higher education" (p. 34).

Pewewardy and Frey's (2004) observation is primarily because smaller percentages of American Indians and Alaska Natives are enrolled in flagship institutions. However, this does not necessarily indicate that indigenous people are not interested in higher education. What also needs to be understood is that for Native people, a bachelor's degree is not always a measure of

TABLE 3.1
Public High School Graduates and Dropouts 2007–08

Race/Ethnicity	Total Graduates[a]	Average Freshman Graduation Rate[b]	Number of Dropouts[c]	Event Dropout Rates[d]
All students	2,900,309		585,496	4.1%
White	1,853,476	81.0%	234,121	2.8%
Total minority	1,046,844		351,375	
Black	415,111	61.5%	159,407	6.7%
Latino/Hispanic	443,328	63.5%	163,389	6.0%
Asian/Pacific Islander	156,687	91.4%	15,576	2.4%
American Indian/ Alaska Native	31,707	64.2%	13,003	7.3%

Note. From *Public School Graduates and Dropouts from the Common Core of Data: School Year 2007–08 (NCES 2010-341),* by R. Stillwell, 2010, Washington, DC: National Center for Education Statistics, Institute of Education Sciences, U.S. Department of Education, http://nces.ed.gov/pubsearch/pubsinfo.asp?pubid=2010341

[a] From Table 2 of the U.S. Department of Education, National Center for Education Statistics, Common Core of Data (CCD), "NCES Common Core of Data State Dropout and Completion Data File," School Year 2007–08, Version 1a. Public high school number of graduates and Averaged Freshman Graduation Rate, by race/ethnicity and state or jurisdiction: School year 2007–08

[b] From Table 2 of the U.S. Department of Education, National Center for Education Statistics, Common Core of Data (CCD), "NCES Common Core of Data State Dropout and Completion Data File," School Year 2007–08, Version 1a. Averaged Freshman Graduation Rate (AFGR) is an estimate of the percentage of an entering freshman class graduating in 4 years. For 2007–08, it equals the total number of diploma recipients in 2007–08 divided by the average membership of the 8th-grade class in 2003–04, the 9th-grade class in 2004–05, and the 10th-grade class in 2005–06.

[c] From Table 6 of the Source U.S. Department of Education, National Center for Education Statistics, Common Core of Data (CCD), "NCES Common Core of Data State Dropout and Completion Data File," School Year 2007–08, Version 1a. Public high school number of dropouts and event dropout rate, by race/ethnicity and state or jurisdiction: School year 2007–08.

[d] The *event dropout* rate is defined as the count of dropouts from a given school year divided by the count of student enrollments within the same grade span at the beginning of the same school year.

success. Success could be an associate of arts or applied science degree from a TCU that enables Indian graduates to secure immediate employment and economic independence for themselves and their families. The lack of high enrollment numbers at mainstream institutions and the propensity to attend TCUs have led to invisibility issues in academe and beyond.

As indicated in the previous section, "(In)visibility," the invisibility of Native Americans has inevitably seeped into higher education (Brayboy, 2004). To undergird this observation, Brayboy and Searle (2007) state that invisibility is also "intimately connected to the ways they [Indians] have been made visible by the government, in schools, and within popular media" (p. 173), and Native Americans face invisibility on a daily basis in all aspects of society beyond their home communities.

In addition, Suina's (1987) assertion that American Indians "are the most underserved and least noticed ethnic group in higher education" (p. 34) still rings true today. Furthermore, we must understand that issues that have an impact on the developmental process of American Indian students are connected to history, self-identification with tribal culture, and the prevalence or relevance of Indian culture in the environment. Lowe (2005) found that the experience of Native Americans in higher education will shape and will be shaped by their Native American identity; thus, the relevance of and respect for indigenous viewpoints is crucial to their success. Kirkness and Barnhardt (1991) also highlight the importance of the perspective of American Indian students and their "need for a higher educational system that *respects* them for who they are, that is *relevant* to their view of the world, that offers *reciprocity* in their relationships with others, and that helps them exercise *responsibility* over their own lives" (p. 1, italics in original). Lee (2009) pushes further by emphasizing that "the importance of education [for indigenous communities] reaches farther than simply a mastery of academic content and critical thinking skills" (p. 20). These are possible factors that contribute to low numbers in the enrollment and graduation rates of American Indians/Alaska Natives, as shown in Tables 3.2–3.4.

TABLE 3.2
American Indian/Native Alaskan College and University Enrollment, Fall 2009

Race/Ethnicity	*Total (in 1,000s)/ % U.S.*	*Male/% U.S.*	*Female/% U.S.*
All students	20,427.7	8,769.5/42.9%	11,658.2/57.1%
White	12,730.8/62.3%	5,594.4/63.8%	7,136.4/61.2%
Total minority	7,012.1/34.3%	2,808.4/32.0%	4,203.7/36.1%
Black	2,919.8/14.3%	1,037.1/11.8%	1,882.7/16.1%
Latino/Hispanic	2,546.7/12.5%	1,066.3/12.2%	1,480.4/12.7%
Asian/Pacific Islander	1,337.7/6.5%	621.5/7.1%	716.1/6.1%
American Indian/ Alaska Native	207.9/1.0%	83.4/1.0%	124.5/1.1%
Non-resident alien	684.8/3.4%	366.7/4.2%	318.1/2.7%

Note. From *Digest of Education Statistics 2011* (NCES 2012-001), by T. D. Snyder & S. A. Dillow, 2012, Washington, DC: National Center for Education Statistics, Institute of Education Sciences, U.S. Department of Education, http://nces.ed.gov/pubs2012/2012001.pdf.

TABLE 3.3
Associate Degrees Conferred in 2010–2011

Race/Ethnicity	Total (in 1,000s)/ % U.S.	Male/% U.S.	Female/% U.S.
All students	849,452/100%	322,916/38.9%	526,536/62.1%
White	552,863/65.1%	216,072/66.9%	336,791/64.0%
Black	113,905/13.4%	36,136/11.2%	77,769/14.8%
Latino/Hispanic	112,211/13.2%	42,232/13.1%	69,979/13.3%
Asian/Pacific Islander	44,021/5.2%	18,264/5.7%	25,757/4.9%
American Indian/ Alaska Native	10,337/1.2%	3,624/1.1% 35% (of American Indian/Alaska Native)	6,713/1.3% 65% (of American Indian/Alaska Native)
Two or more races	16,115/1.9%	6,588/2.0%	9,527/1.8%
Nonresident alien	849,452/100%	322,916/38.9%	526,536/62.1%

Note. From *Digest of Education Statistics 2011* (NCES 2012-001), by T. D. Snyder & S. A. Dillow, 2012, Washington, DC: National Center for Education Statistics, Institute of Education Sciences, U.S. Department of Education, http://nces.ed.gov/pubs2012/2012001.pdf.

TABLE 3.4
Bachelor's Degrees Conferred in 2009–2010

Race/Ethnicity	Total (in 1,000s)/ % U.S.	Male/% U.S.	Female/% U.S.
All students	1,650,014/100%	706,633/42.7%	943,381/57.3%
White	1,167,499/70.8%	513,717/72.7%	653,782/69.3%
Black	164,844/10.0%	56,171/7.9%	108,673/11.5%
Latino/Hispanic	140,316/8.5%	55,092/7.8%	85,224/9.0%
Asian/Pacific Islander	117,422/7.1%	53,377/7.6%	64,045/6.8%
American Indian/ Alaska Native	12,399/0.8%	4.875/0.7%	7,524/0.8%
Nonresident alien[a]	47,534/2.9%	23,401/3.3%	24,133/2.6%

Note. From *Digest of Education Statistics 2011* (NCES 2012-001), by T. D. Snyder & S. A. Dillow, 2012, Washington, DC: National Center for Education Statistics, Institute of Education Sciences, U.S. Department of Education, http://nces.ed.gov/pubs2012/2012001.pdf.
[a]Nonresident alien percentage distribution is not included with the U.S. citizen count.

Intergenerational Trauma

At the heart of this new field is a simple but contentious idea—that genes have a "memory." That the lives of your grandparents—the air they breathed, the food they ate, even the things they saw—can directly affect you, decades later, despite your never experiencing these things yourself. And that what you do in your lifetime could in turn affect your grandchildren.
("The Ghost in Your Genes," 2006)

Intergenerational or historical trauma has been a controversial topic for non-Native people because there is an accepted notion that what happened in the past is in the past. However, scientific research in epigenetics has begun to demonstrate that intergenerational trauma is real, that it has an impact on present-day populations, and it will have effects on future generations.[11] Native healers, medicine people, and elders have always known this, and it is common knowledge in Native oral traditions. Brayboy (2004) uses TribalCrit to emphasize this by stating, "Stories are not separate from theory; they make up theory and are, therefore, real and legitimate sources of data and ways of being" (p. 430). This is crucial to understanding the detrimental results of European colonization for it dismantled many indigenous communities' egalitarian way of life. Indigenous women and men were equal partners in all aspects of Native life such as labor, economic authority, political power, and spiritual ways. Native feminist scholars such as Mishuana R. Goeman (Goeman & Denetdale, 2009), Luana Ross (2009), Kim Anderson (2001), Lisa K. Hall (2009), Angela W. Waziyatawin (2003), Dian Million (2009), Renya K. Ramirez (2009), Audra Simpson (2009), Jennifer Nez Denetdale (2009), Sarah Deer (2009), and others provide insightful analysis on how American Indian men are dealing with challenges and how some are unfortunately contributing to continued oppression of their communities. We use TribalCrit to help better understand how Native American males succumbed to White male privilege: master and slave, conquerer and conquered. In addition, Brayboy (2004) asserts that TribalCrit "values narrative and stories as important sources of data" (p. 428), and this is crucial in understanding the power of oral traditions. The work of Native feminist scholars strongly illustrates the importance of this emerging field's impact on Native American men and American society's accepted notions of heteronormative patriarchy.

In "Securing Navajo National Boundaries: War, Patriotism, Tradition, and the Diné Marriage Act of 2005," Denetdale (2009) discusses how tradition has been used to validate contemporary attitudes and practices with the overall goal of upholding American imperialism and colonialism. Through her analysis of how some Navajo traditions are evoked to reinforce imperialism and colonialism, Denetdale illustrates the struggles for American Indian women and men in the 21st century:

> Just as victims of trauma (such as those held hostage) suffer physical, sexual, or emotional abuse or cult indoctrination, so have Native peoples exhibited an emotional bonding with their conquerors. Of this tendency to deny the oppressions under which we live as Native peoples, Waziyatawin (2003) wrote, "While this might be a way to overcome powerlessness and maintain hope in an overwhelming situation, it nonetheless denies the violence of the perpetrator. Or, perhaps some rationalize the abuser's violence as a way to maintain an emotional and psychological bond with the colonizer in the face of an ongoing colonization." Thus, the colonizers coerced and used violence against Navajos to compel them to adopt American beliefs, attitudes, and practices. . . . Certainly, Navajos' uncritical acceptance of American values and the ways in which they have aligned contemporary Navajo beliefs and practices with tradition can be seen in the blurring of American and Navajo values. (p. 145)

These struggles provide some context for why American Indian men have educational disparities in higher education. From this work we hope to ask future generations of Native Americans, Where are you going to college? instead of, Are you going to college?

Up to this point, much of the challenges Native Americans face have been analyzed using CRT and TribalCrit. We use TribalCrit to help better understand how Native American males can address historical trauma by honoring and relying on oral history. The detrimental result of conquest was that Native men's traditional roles were greatly diminished, as they were no longer *warriors*, meaning protectors or providers. Another result was that Native American men were subjected to humiliation and emasculation, and Native women did not understand why their men could not stand up to White oppressors. Thus, Native men were facing a vise with pressures from both sides—Native women and colonizers. They also had to deal with White influences and mechanisms of domination, such as liquor, superiority measures, and jingoistic platitudes, which manifested themselves in the "hang around the fort" syndrome.[12] The long-term effect of being conquered had demoralized Native men. One result of this has been a tendency to shy away from education. Native women, on the other hand, are becoming empowered through education.

In Grey's (2003–2004) analysis of *Patriarchy as a Colonial Construct*, she reiterates Beatrice Medicine's assertion that "in the face of coerced agrarianism and the attending devaluation of hunting and the consequences of forced removal and relocation, Native men have suffered a loss of status and traditional self-sufficiency even more extensive than their female counterparts" (p. 13). Grey further states, "Rather than the gender equality sought by feminists, Aboriginal women most often speak of the goal of gender harmony" (p. 13). Grey also refers to Fernandez's (2003) observation that "gender balance strengthens our circles; the values and teachings show us that women occupy one side of the circle and men occupy the other. The vision is not to make one better than the other, but to show how they are complementary" (p. 254).

We now turn to what was usually expected of Native men and their struggle to maintain traditional roles and connections in contemporary society. Each American Indian man has a foundational image representing what it means to be an American Indian man, especially his roles and expectations. This foundation is based on a man's spirituality, physicality, common way of life, and social interactions. Most important, spirituality explains a man's existential appearance as it directs a man toward positive energies in the world to experience happiness and laughter. Through this positive outlook, he develops a good attitude, emotions, thoughts, and behavior to enjoy life. Thus, his outlook on life and the path he takes comes from his spiritual ways.

Each Native American man will learn different things based on his culture. What is not different for each Native American man is his understanding of what is expected of him as a man; his role in the community; and the connection he has with other men, women, children, the earth, and the universe.

Some traditional specific roles for Native American men included hunting, farming, and working with women to sustain life. Native men were teachers, storytellers, traders, protectors, hunters, farmers, and doctors, and many fulfill other roles specifically designed for them to sustain the community. These men learned and used various thoughts, ideas, ways, and tools to ensure life for their families and communities. Native American communities also include *two-spirit* people—gays, lesbians, and transgendered people. For example, in Navajo culture, there are multiple genders: male, female, and *nádleeh*. The nádleeh are two-spirit people who are part of the culture in "an ever-dynamic cycle of feminine and masculine forces inherent within all creation" (Estrada, 2011, p. 171). Estrada describes Lydia Nibley's documentary film *Two Spirits* as one that "invites a gender-balanced understanding of the nature of Navajo cosmology in which nádleeh exist as a natural reflection of the cycle of male and female inherent in all aspects of the universe" (p. 171). While most of the knowledge base that Native men possess comes from their communities, European, American, and other peoples influenced how they should view their roles and expectations as well as masculinities.

Rites of Passage and Challenges

Through the contemporary heteronormative and patriarchal lenses, success means a person should possess a college degree to be viewed as an educated, cultured, and contributing citizen to American and global society, but for indigenous people, there are alternative pathways to success. Native American men learn a significant amount of cultural knowledge when they participate in a rite of passage or puberty ceremony. For many Native nations, a rite of passage for males occurs around the time a boy's voice starts to change. The main lesson in the rite of passage is for the boy to learn the necessary skills and knowledge to live in this world and to work for the well-being of his family and community.

Each Native nation conducts its rite of passage ceremony differently; however, there are similarities in terms of goals and pedagogy. Native American boys train prior to a puberty ceremony, and as the boy transforms from child to adolescent his family and relatives prepare him for the ceremony and life. Depending on the Native community, a puberty ceremony can take a day, several days, a month, or an entire year. A boy's puberty ceremony in many Native communities involves mostly the male relations of the boy's extended family. The boy will go through physical, spiritual, emotional, and psychological challenges. He will learn from all these challenges and use the knowledge to help him on his path as a young Native American man and beyond. He will have a better understanding of his roles, responsibilities, expectations, and obligations to himself, family, and community. To provide an example, Oscar Tso describes his puberty ceremony in Maureen Trudelle Schwarz's (1997) *Molded in the Image of Changing Woman: Navajo Views on the Human Body and Personhood*:

> They built a sweat for me, and they talked to me about my responsibilities as a man. And then, what I need to do to take care of myself. They talked about how I should be when I get married. What should I know and how I should be towards a woman, because I have a mother, I have sisters. And I have to have respect for my mother, my sisters and then have that same respect for a woman that I will marry. And then all the daughters that I will have, or granddaughters that I will have. So, those kinds of things are explained to you. And then about how you need to keep yourself real strong, try to stay with one woman for a long time, you know. Have a set of children. And they can really preach, you know, and talk to you about a lot of things. And those are some things that are explained to boys. And then, how you have to be strong, what kind of herbs you have to take from time to time to purify and cleanse your body. To keep your mind and body strong, and have a sense of purpose as you go about living this life. So, I had the sweat done for me, as well as the Beauty Way, the Hoozhonee done for me. (p. 159)

Tso and other Native American boys who participate in a sweat learn cultural teachings, life's complexities, and sincerity with humor. Herbs such as tobacco, sweetgrass, cedar, or sage are also used in many American Indian rites of passage.

Through such ceremonies, a young boy learns songs, prayers, stories, and ways to live a healthy life. He learns how to balance his physical, emotional, psychological, and spiritual self. The puberty ceremony strengthens and guides a male's adult life and ensures that a young Native boy lives a long and prosperous life for himself, his family, and his community. Native American boys and men are not alone in trying to sustain the family and community. Native American girls and women are equal partners, for they also have roles, expectations, and obligations and participate in puberty ceremonies to learn what it means to be a woman. They, too, understand what it means to live a balanced way of life.

To that end, numerous Native American women scholars, such as Goeman and Denetdale (2009), Ross (2009), Anderson (2001), Million (2009), Ramirez (2009), Simpson (2009), Denetdale (2009), and Deer (2009), are examining Native American gender responsibilities, rites of passage, gender relations in Native communities, and the history of Native women in terms of patriarchy and its effects on families. Their contributions can help illuminate how Native men are dealing with many socioeconomic challenges. In Dian Million's (2009) "Felt Theory: An Indigenous Feminist Approach to Affect and History," she argues that Canadian First Nation women's first-person and experiential narratives were political acts that countered accounts of Canadian and U.S. colonial histories. These counternarratives were strengths for women and provide examples of possible resolutions to many of life's challenges, like educational disparity. Million states:

> Canada and the United States resisted the truth in the emotional content of this felt knowledge: colonialism as it is *felt* by those who experience it. Ending the silence in the communities was a significant political action. This would not be fully appreciated until the residential school narratives had explosively shaken Canada by the late 1980s and early 1990s as the same communities began to narrate the larger systematic attack that had been perpetrated on both their minds and their bodies. In between were years in which women honed and developed a profound literature of experience. (p. 58)

This excerpt indicates how Native women use narrative as a tool to battle the challenges they face in their own communities and the nation–state. Native men learn from these narratives that their silence or compliance contributed to the continued oppression and patriarchy of their communities, which include women and men. This oppression has not dissipated and remains to be resolved. Moreover, some of the educational disparities result from Native American men choosing not to go to college, not following through on a commitment or goal they may have set for themselves or that their families have set for them. In fact, some Native American men view higher education or education in general as being for women, thus explaining the lack of motivation and the absence of any sense of responsibility and obligation some Native American men feel with respect to education.

Recommendations and Plausible Prescriptions

What we present may paint a somewhat dismal picture, but there is hope for Native Americans in college, especially for males. In the following sections we present ways to increase the recruitment, retention, and graduation of Native American men. First, we discuss the crucial role of support systems and advocates for Native Americans in higher education. Second, we highlight the work national organizations are engaged in for Native men. Third, we discuss how TCUs can be instrumental in addressing the crisis Native American men face. Finally, we discuss the need for Native people and communities to look within their cultures for remedies and guidance for the crisis facing Native men.

Native American Programs and Native American Studies

In a study of the Harvard Native American Program (NAP), it was found that the NAP provided a space that enhanced the educational experiences of all students who sought out its services (Bitsóí, 2007). In addition, this study illuminated the important role the NAP played in providing successful college experiences for Native students at Harvard College. Other institutions, for example, Cornell, Dartmouth, and Stanford, have NAPs and affinity housing for Native American students that are instrumental in the students' success. In addition, HeavyRunner and DeCelles (2002) address the need for family-oriented environments in postsecondary education in their family education model for American Indian students. Similar research studies, including Jackson and Smith's (2001), stress the importance of creating a Native community in colleges and universities to create a home away from home for Native Americans as a way to help them achieve success in higher education. This is in line with Rindone's (1988) finding that family is the key to the academic success of high-achieving Indian students. Thus, finding a sense of place, family, and belonging within higher education is instrumental in Native American student success.

Some institutions have taken further steps to institutionalize NAPs and NAS departments by creating senior administrative roles for Native American/American Indian Programs. For example, there are special advisers to the president for Native American affairs at the University of New Mexico, Arizona State University, Northern Arizona University, and the University of Arizona. It should be noted that at the University of Arizona, the special adviser position was elevated to vice presidential status, which demonstrates the institutional commitment there. These important administrators are constantly advocating for Native Americans and have created innovative ways to recruit, retain, and graduate Native American students. The models warrant further investigation for effective practices that can be shared with the rest of academe.

Beacons of Hope

While few national organizations and programs specifically focus their efforts on Native American males, we highlight a few that have begun to address issues Native youths face. These examples can serve as resources for Native thought leaders to assist in making inroads with their efforts to restore confidence and pride in their youths.

National Indian Youth Leadership Project

The National Indian Youth Leadership Project (NIYLP) was established "to nurture the potential of Native youth to be contributors to a more positive world through adventure-based learning and service to family, community, and nature" (NIYLP, 2008). Furthermore, NIYLP leadership envisions "a world with generations of healthy, capable, caring, resilient Native youth who contribute to their groups, families, communities, and nations" (2008). NIYLP is unique for Native youth because of its Tacheeh Project, designed "especially for adolescent boys in the transition to manhood" (NIYLP, 2008) through the use of a *tach'eeh*, or sweat lodge ceremony. NIYLP administrators stress the importance of the Tacheeh Project and describe its efforts as follows:

> Tach'eeh is an important aspect of Navajo culture promoting both a traditional structure and rite of passage ceremony for young males. The teachings of the Tach'eeh ceremony are incorporated into the program. These teachings deal with birth, abstinence, self-control and respect for females; and include qualities—such as strength and endurance—of becoming a positive and productive male. Additional emphasis is placed on instilling a commitment to nature as a contribution to one's home, school and community.

Center for Native American Youth, Aspen Institute

The Center for Native American Youth (CNAY, 2011a) at the Aspen Institute is "dedicated to improving the health, safety, and overall well-being of Native American youth through communication, policy development, and advocacy." The CNAY (2011b) fulfills its mission by

- Communicating about the challenges Native youth face and best practices on how to respond to those challenges;
- Providing technical assistance to tribal governments, tribal organizations and Native American programs for grant management, as well as program development and implementation;
- Identifying and assisting tribes with securing available federal and private funding; and
- Monitoring youth-related activities, especially suicide prevention efforts, and encouraging replication of successful programs.

Furthermore, CNAY (2011c) collects narratives from Native youth "to share stories of motivation, overcoming barriers, reaching goals, and Native Pride" so that "youth can be creative in their storytelling and these submissions will help empower and support young Natives everywhere." According to a participant, "We may be the products of a hurt people in history, but we are the seeds of restoration for today and many years to come. We can be the generation to defeat those hardships" (CNAY, 2011c).

Native American Fatherhood and Families Association

The mission of the Native American Fatherhood and Families Association (NAFFA, 2012b) is "to strengthen families by responsibly involving fathers in the lives of their children, families and communities and partnering with mothers to provide happy and safe families." Through its training programs, NAFFA uses "a culturally rich model that inspires and motivates Fathers and Mothers to devote their best efforts in teaching and raising children to develop the potential and attributes needed for successful living" (NAFFA, 2012a). The following are key principles of the training program:

- It is important that real and lasting change comes from within.
- Our program inspires and ignites self-motivation through natural techniques in bringing change to a person.
- Understanding one's self worth and the value they bring to their family will change their very nature, drawing them closer to loved ones.

- We must be a forward thinking, forward looking and forward moving people.
- When we truly understand the past it should inspire and motivate us to work toward a richer, better future. This is accomplished through strong fathers and mothers who are devoted to strengthening their families. (NAFFA, 2012a)

While these organizations are engaged in wonderful and productive practices for Native American youths, we call for a program or center specifically for Native American males. To that end, two excellent programs that could serve as a guide for such a national program are Call Me MISTER ("Welcome to Call Me MISTER," 2012) at Clemson University and Project MALES ("Project MALES: Mentoring to Achieve Latino Educational Success," n.d.) at the University of Texas at Austin. By using these programs as models, we envision the creation of a program that is culturally appropriate and responsive to Native American men who seek to achieve their educational goals.

TCUs

According to the American Indian Higher Education Consortium (AIHEC, 2012),

> TCUs were created in response to the higher education needs of American Indians and generally serve geographically isolated populations that have no other means of accessing education beyond the high school level. TCUs have become increasingly important to educational opportunity for Native American students and are unique institutions that combine personal attention with cultural relevance to encourage American Indians— especially those living on reservations—to overcome the barriers they face to higher education.

Because of the mission of TCUs, we believe they can play a critical role in helping Native American communities address the challenges facing Native American men as they attempt to successfully complete college. As AIHEC (2012) notes, TCUs are culturally unique in higher education opportunities because "all parts of the colleges' curricula are designed from an American Indian perspective, and the individual courses reflect this effort. The colleges offer courses in tribal languages that might otherwise disappear, as well as other traditional subjects."

Since TCUs are purveyors of indigenous languages and sometimes serve as stewards of cultural knowledge and traditions, we recommend that Native communities begin to work with them to restore cultural identity, even more so to allow for a renewal in understanding the importance of the gender role balance. For example,

> All students at Oglala Lakota College are required to take courses offered by the Lakota Studies Department, which provides a cultural focus for the entire college. The department offers community workshops, helps collect materials relevant to tribal history and culture, and is integral in efforts to maintain the Lakota language. (AIHEC, 2012)

While not all tribal nations have a TCU, establishing programs targeted to Native American men at current TCUs could serve as an example for Native communities.

Cultural Remedies

> *If you live right, you will live a long life. . . . There is strength in the Indian way of life.*
> (Chosa, 2011, p. 55)

While TCUs are doing an exceptional job for Native communities and students, we urge the full participation of tribal communities at all levels—grandparents, parents, children, educators, leaders, and government—to earnestly and intentionally look within their cultural capital to find answers to address this educational crisis. In our recommendation for Native Americans to tap into their cultures for answers, we again turn to Grey's (2003–2004) call for tradition renewal: "With an acknowledged goal of renewing tradition (in which gender roles were interdependent), it follows that Native women require the participation of men in the social, political and spiritual life of the community" (p. 14). Thus, we are not calling for a return to the traditional cultural ways practiced before European contact, as gender roles and expectations have changed over time, but we call for reinvigorating the cultural knowledge base for guiding boys into becoming men in these contemporary times. We are aware that Native people are losing their languages and to some extent their cultures, so a resurgence in language and culture programs is imperative. This way Native children can be bilingual and bicultural. Deacon, Pendley, Hinson, & Hinson (2011) states,

> It has recently been found that biculturalism (i.e., the ability [of a minority group] to adapt to majority cultural norms while still remaining grounded in one's own culture) serves to buffer [American Indian] youth against negative outcomes such as substance abuse. It is believed that bicultural competence allows these youth to combine what is best from both cultures as a source of strength in the face of adversity. (p. 58)

Conclusion

History is important to Native Americans, for it tells us of our creation, who we are, what we have endured, and reminds us of what we have learned to determine our future. What we as Native Americans have experienced since European contact continues to have an impact and to influence our communities in the United States. History has had an impact on the education of Native people, and as a result Native men continue to lag behind in higher education as fewer graduate with an associate's degree or higher.

What can institutions and individuals do to change this? We suggest that cultural remedies provide a way to help alleviate educational disparities and socioeconomic challenges. A specific remedy for Native males would be the restoration and celebration of the rites of passage through ceremony. Not very many Native American men have gone through a rite of passage in the 21st century, so Native communities will need to revitalize and regenerate a rite of passage for boys. While some communities are doing exactly this, every Native American community needs to implement a systematic way for young boys to participate in a rite of passage so they will learn the responsibilities and obligations they have to themselves, their families, and their communities, and perhaps most important, they will learn the value of language and culture. Furthermore, our future men will learn what it means to commit to a goal and to achieve it.

Native people have always known that it takes a village to raise a child, so male relatives and men in the community usually conduct a rite of passage in many Native communities. These males serve as role models for families and communities and assist with the nurturing and development of boys to men. Therefore, the community and institutions (tribal elders, healers, medicine people, and parents) need to develop role model programs in which Native American men who are successful in life in terms of education, career, family, parenting, and commitment are spotlighted and looked to for assistance with developing and strengthening healthy families. The number of Native American men who are successful in any of these areas may be minimal, and the number of role models small, but the establishment of such programs is imperative. Moreover, Native American communities, colleges, and institutions need to develop national programs and networks so that Native students who attend college see others from their communities and other Native communities who are successful in these environments.

In addition to acquiring cultural knowledge, Native American men can go to college and graduate with the help of a mentoring or coaching program. Native American men, and men in general, usually listen to what other men have to say when it comes to life and the challenges they deal with on a daily basis. Colleges and universities need to develop an approach on how to encourage Native American men to be mentors to men entering college. The program's structure should be determined by the institution and, possibly, the Native American communities that send their children to the school. In addition, the role of Native women should be emphasized in Native communities because they can play instrumental roles in such mentoring efforts.

Colleges and universities also need to make an intentional commitment to Native American education. They need to demonstrate what is necessary for Native American children to succeed and graduate. How can this be done? Each college or university must determine the methodology, but one approach to consider is for the college or university administrators to enter into a dialogue with members of the Native American communities that send their children to the school so both know exactly what each can do for the students. A financial commitment is also necessary on the part of the college or university. Without a financial commitment, the good intentions of colleges or universities will not increase the graduation rates of Native American men, and the communities will see the institutions as supporting their students only with words.

Another way colleges and universities can show their commitment to Native American students is by creating a center or home on campus. Some institutions, such as New Mexico State University, Fort Lewis College, Northern Arizona University, Cornell, Dartmouth, and Stanford, provide Native American centers or residence halls where Native American students can congregate in a central location on campus. Cocurricular activities, such as meetings, study sessions, dinners, and other social events for Native students, provide a welcoming environment that is crucial to an effective support system that they can turn to in times of need and celebration.

Primary and secondary education systems also need to make a commitment to the educational success of Native American children. Many Native American children do not graduate from high school for a variety of reasons, but usually the cause is socioeconomic challenges. Many who do graduate do not consider attending college because of their lack of confidence and preparation, lack of understanding of the college admission process, and lack of financial literacy necessary to navigate the frustrating and convoluted financial aid process. Elementary, middle, and high school administrators need to develop support programs such as mentoring initiatives, college preparatory curricula, tutoring, and test preparation workshops. Officials of schools located on Native American reservations or schools that serve a significant percentage of Native American students need to work with their leaders in government, education, and local school boards to collaborate with colleges and universities to develop support programs so Native American students are able to learn what college is about and how they can continue their education as undergraduates and graduate students.

Native people should not look to the education system as a panacea. They should invest in their languages and cultural knowledge bases. It is encouraging that Native American language revitalization movements are emerging across the country. These efforts should be highlighted and supported even more than they are now by national Native advocacy groups and tribal leaders. These efforts will certainly allow Native children to become bilingual (and bicultural), particularly since bilingualism has been shown to be a good indicator of school success for Native American students. Thus, Native American communities will need to establish and implement Native language tests, programs, schools, workshops, and institutes sustained by Native communities to demonstrate cultural pride in Native languages.

It is known that given an even playing field anyone can attend and graduate from college. This is true for Native American men, and it will take a collective effort to increase the retention and graduation rates of Native men. Colleges, universities, and Native American communities are all important in figuring out how to do this in the 21st century. A dialogue is necessary for all stakeholders involved in all realms to develop plausible ways to address and overcome educational disparities for Native American men. While colonization and imperialism continue to have a deleterious impact on Native Americans, acknowledging and understanding this impact will empower Native communities to address social challenges using a strengths-based approach. With this type of approach, the goal of Native American men attending and graduating from college can be attained through K–12 schools, colleges, universities, and Native American communities working together. Overall, this collaborative effort will be rewarded with an increased number of Native Americans attending and graduating from higher education institutions.

Notes

1. Like other indigenous scholars, we use the following terms interchangeably in this chapter: *American Indians, Native Americans, Natives, Indians, indigenous peoples,* and *tribal nations. Native* is often used to refer to Native culture; however, tribal affiliation has greater importance than broad terminology (Herring, 1991). The diversity among tribes makes tribal affiliation a more accurate and descriptive self-identification.

2. American Indian reservations are a result of the federal government's primary motivation to control and socially engineer the assimilation and deculturalization of American Indians into White society (Spring, 2009; Takaki, 1993).

3. Sovereignty is essential to the development of tribal nations regarding education, economic development, social services, and health care (Begay, 1997; Bitsóí, 2007).

4. Traditional governance was egalitarian, but federal policies have forced tribal nations to elect a president or chairman. However, today "tribal governments are at times focused on efforts to maintain their culture and the community values of their tribal nation" (Torres & Bitsóí, 2011, p. 172).

5. According to the American Indian Movement (AIM, n.d.), "AIM (the American Indian Movement) began in Minneapolis, Minnesota, in the summer of 1968. It began taking form when 200 people from the Indian community turned out for a meeting called by a group of Native American community activists led by George Mitchell, Dennis Banks, and Clyde Bellecourt. Frustrated by discrimination and decades of federal Indian policy, they came together to discuss the critical issues restraining them and to take control over their own destiny. Out of that ferment and determination, the American Indian Movement was born."

6. After the Indian Colleges at Harvard and William and Mary were closed down, no American Indians enrolled at either school until much, much later (Belgarde, 1996).

7. According to the report, "The Indian educational enterprise is peculiarly in need of the kind of approach that recognizes this principle: that is, less concerned with a conventional school system and more with the understanding of human beings. It is impossible to visit Indian schools without feeling that on the whole they have been less touched than have better public schools by the newer knowledge of human behavior; that they reflect, for the most part, an attitude toward children characteristic of older city schools or of rural schools in backward sections; that they are distinctly below the accepted social and educational standards of school systems in most cities and the better rural communities" ("Meriam Report," 1928, p. 346).

8. "Contrary to what some believe, the Indian was never Dartmouth's official mascot. The use of the Indian in conjunction with Dartmouth's athletic teams dated back to the 1920s. It is difficult to determine exactly why, but some Boston sportswriters and cartoonists began to refer to Dartmouth's teams as the Indians prior to the 1922 football game with Harvard. The use of the 'Indian' nickname remained in use informally and unofficially until the early 1970s. In 1974, Dartmouth's Board of Trustees issued a statement calling for an end to the use of the Indian as a mascot" ("Ask Dartmouth: Student Life," 2012). Until the board's intervention, the use of the Indian as a mascot, unofficial or not, was a prime example of the paternalism and patriarchal aims of White (college) men's desire to control the image of Native Americans.

9. See Carney's (1999) description of the three colleges and their charters that specifically called for the education of indigenous peoples.
10. The National Museum of the American Indian (NMAI) is an excellent resource dedicated to dispelling stereotypes. Part of the mission of the NMAI is "acting as a resource for the hemisphere's Native communities and to serving the greater public as an honest and thoughtful conduit to Native cultures—present and past—in all their richness, depth, and diversity" (NMAI, 2012).
11. "Epigenetics adds a whole new layer to genes beyond the DNA. It proposes a control system of 'switches' that turn genes on or off—and suggests that things people experience, like nutrition and stress, can control these switches and cause heritable effects in humans" ("The Ghost in Your Genes," 2006).
12. *Hang around the fort* refers to "those Indian leaders in the nineteenth century who moved close to governmental installations and cooperated with the federal government" usually to receive meager supplies to survive rather than continue with traditional lifestyles of hunting and gathering for their sustenance (Smith & Warrior, 1996, p. 136).

References

American Indian Higher Education Consortium. (2012). *About AIHEC.* Retrieved July 5, 2012, from http://www.aihec.org/about/index.cfm

American Indian Movement (AIM). (n.d.). *American Indian Movement.* Minnesota Historical Society Library, Retrieved January 14, 2014, from http://libguides.mnhs.org/aim.

Anderson, K. (2001). *A recognition of being: Reconstructing Native womanhood.* Toronto, Ontario, Canada: Sumach Press.

Ask Dartmouth: Student life. (2012). Retrieved October 20, 2012, from http://ask.dartmouth.edu/categories/stulife/19.html

Banks, J. A. (1993). The canon debate, knowledge construction, and multicultural education. *Educational Researcher, 22*(5), 4–14.

Begay, M. A., Jr. (1997). *Leading by choice, not chance: Leadership education for native chief executives of American Indian nations* (Unpublished doctoral dissertation). Harvard University, Cambridge, MA.

Belgarde, W. L. (1996). History of American Indian community colleges. In C. Turner, M. Garcia, A. Nora, & L. I. Rendon (Eds.), *Racial & ethnic diversity in higher education* (2nd ed., pp. 3–13). Boston, MA: Pearson Custom Publishing.

Bitsóí, L. L. (2007). *Native leaders in the new millennium: An examination of success factors of Native American males at Harvard College* (Unpublished doctoral dissertation). University of Pennsylvania, Philadelphia, PA.

Boyer, P. (1997). *Native American colleges: Progress and prospects.* Princeton, NJ: Carnegie Foundation for the Advancement of Teaching.

Brayboy, B. M. J. (2004). Hiding in the ivy: American Indian students and visibility in elite educational settings. *Harvard Educational Review, 74*(2), 125–152.

Brayboy, B. M. J. (2006). Toward a tribal critical race theory in education. *Urban Review, 37*(5), 425–446.

Brayboy, B. M., & Searle, K. A. (2007). Thanksgiving and serial killers: Representations of American Indians in schools. In S. Books (Ed.), *Invisible children in the society and its schools* (3rd ed., pp. 173–192). Mahwah, NJ: Erlbaum.

Bureau of Indian Affairs. (2012). *Bureau of Indian affairs.* Retrieved July 6, 2012, from http://www.bia.gov/WhatWeDo/index.htm

Carney, C. M. (1999). *Native American higher education in the United States.* New Brunswick, NJ: Transaction Publishers.

Center for Native American Youth. (2011a). *About us: Overview.* Retrieved October 10, 2013, from http://cnay.org/AboutOverview.html

Center for Native American Youth. (2011b). *Our work: Overview.* Retrieved October 10, 2013, from http://cnay.org/OurWorkOverview.html

Center for Native American Youth. (2011c). *Stories of inspiration.* Retrieved October 10, 2013, from http://cnay.org/StoriesofInspiration.html

Chosa, J. (2011). Respect the Indian way of life. *Oshkaabewis Native Journal, 8*(1), 55–57.

Deacon, Z., Pendley, J., Hinson, W. R., & Hinson, J. D. (2011). Chokka-chaffa'kilimpi', chikashshiyaakni'kilimpi: Strong family, strong nation. *American Indian and Alaska Native Mental Health Research, 18*(2), 41–63.

Deer, S. (2009). Decolonizing rape law: A Native feminist synthesis of safety and sovereignty. *Wicazo Sa Review, 24*(2), 149–167.

Denetdale, J. (2009). Securing Navajo national boundaries: War, patriotism, tradition, and the Diné Marriage Act of 2005. *Wicazo Sa Review, 24*(2), 131–148.

Diné College. (2012). *History.* Retrieved July 16, 2012, from http://www.dinecollege.edu/about/history.php

Estrada, G. (2011). Two spirits, Nádleeh, and LGBTQ2 Navajo gaze. *American Indian Culture and Research Journal, 35*(4), 167–190.

Evans, N. J., Forney, D. S., & Guido-DiBrito, F. (1998). *Student development in college: Theory, research, and practice.* San Francisco, CA: Jossey-Bass.

Fernandez, C. (2003). Coming full circle: A young man's perspective on building gender equality in aboriginal communities. In K. Anderson & B. Lawrence (Eds.), *Strong woman stories: Native vision and community survival* (pp. 242–254). Toronto, Ontario, Canada: Sumach Press.

The ghost in your genes. (2006). Retrieved October 10, 2013, from http://www.bbc.co.uk/sn/tvradio/programmes/horizon/ghostgenes.shtml

Goeman, M. (2011). Introduction to indigenous performances: Upsetting the terrains of settler colonialism. *American Indian Culture and Research Journal, 35*(4), 4–18.

Goeman, M., & Denetdale, J. N. (2009). Native feminisms: Legacies, interventions, and indigenous sovereignties. *Wicazo Sa Review, 24*(2), 9–13.

Grey, S. (2003–2004). Decolonising feminism: Aboriginal women and the global "sisterhood." *Enweyin: The Way We Speak, 8*, 9–22.

Guardia, J. R., & Evans, N. J. (2008). Student development in tribal colleges and universities. *NASPA Journal, 45*(2), 237–264.

Hall, L. K. (2009). Navigating our own "Sea of Islands": Remapping a theoretical space for Hawaiian women and indigenous feminism. *Wicazo Sa Review, 24*(2), 15–38.

HeavyRunner, I., & DeCelles, R. (2002). Family education model: Meeting the student retention challenge. *Journal of American Indian Education, 41*(2), 29–37.

Herring, R. D. (1991). Counseling indigenous American youth. In C. C. Lee (Ed.), *Multicultural issues in counseling: New approaches to diversity* (2nd ed., pp. 53–70). Alexandria, VA: American Association for Counseling and Development.

Indian Reorganization Act of 1934. (2013). *25 U.S.C. Subchapter V—Protection of Indians and conservation of resources.* Retrieved October 10, 2013, from http://www.gpo.gov/fdsys/pkg/USCODE-2011-title25/html/USCODE-2011-title25-chap14-subchapV.htm

Indian Reorganization Act, 48 Stat. 984, 25 U.S.C. § 461 *et seq.* (1934).

Jackson, A. P., & Smith, S. A. (2001). Postsecondary transitions among Navajo Indians. *Journal of American Indian Education, 40*(2), 28–47.

Journell, W. (2009). An incomplete history: Representation of American Indians in state social studies standards. *Journal of American Indian Education, 48*(2), 18–32.

Kirkness, V. J., & Barnhardt, R. (1991). First Nations and higher education: The four Rs—respect, relevance, reciprocity, responsibility. *Journal of American Indian Education, 30*(3), 1–15.

Ladson-Billings, G. (2003). *Critical race theory perspectives on the social studies: The profession, policies, and curriculum.* Greenwich, CT: Information Age.

Lee, T. S. (2009). Building Native nations through Native students' commitment to their communities. *Journal of American Indian Education, 48*(1), 19–36.

Lowe, S. C. (2005). This is who I am: Experiences of Native American students. *New Directions for Student Services: Serving Native American Students, 109*, 33–40.

Mazzetti, M., Cooper, H., & Baker, P. (2011). Behind the hunt for Bin Laden. *The New York Times.* Retrieved October 10, 2013, from http://www.nytimes.com/2011/05/03/world/asia/03intel.html?_r=2&adxnnl=1&adxnnlx=1381875794-6pAIxFymk0AuiwFEyWDe4w

McClellan, G. S., Fox, M. J. T., & Lowe, S. C. (2005). Where we have been: A history of Native American higher education. *New Directions for Student Services: Serving Native American Students, 109*, 17–32.

McDonald, J. D. (1992). *Attitudinal factors affecting academic success of American Indian college students: The development of the Native American college student attitude scale* (Unpublished doctoral dissertation). University of South Dakota, Vermillion, SD.

Meriam Report. (1928). *Meriam report: The problem of Indian administration (1921).* Retrieved July 3, 2013, from Native American Rights Fund National Indian Law Library website: http://www.narf.org/nill/resources/meriam.htm

Million, D. (2009). Felt theory: An indigenous feminist approach to affect and history. *Wicazo Sa Review, 24*(2), 53–76.

National Congress of American Indians. (2013). *Tribal governance*. Retrieved July 5, 2012, from http://www.ncai.org/policy-issues/tribal-governance

National Indian Youth Leadership Project. (2008). *Welcome to NIYLP*. Retrieved October 10, 2013, from http://www.niylp.org/mission-vision.htmhttp://www.niylp.org/

National Indian Youth Leadership Project. (2008). *The Tacheeh Project: A program for young men*. Retrieved October 10, 2013, from http://www.niylp.org/projects/tacheeh.htm

National Museum of the American Indian. (2012). *Mission statement*. Retrieved October 10, 2013, from http://nmai.si.edu/about/mission/

Native American Fatherhood and Families Association. (2012a). *Fatherhood/motherhood is sacred*. Retrieved October 10, 2013, from http://aznaffa.org/fatherhood-motherhood.html

Native American Fatherhood and Families Association. (2012b). *Native American Fatherhood and Families Association*. Retrieved October 10, 2013, from http://aznaffa.org/

Nelson, R. M. (2013). *A guide to Native American studies programs in the United States and Canada*. Retrieved October 10, 2013, from https://facultystaff.richmond.edu/~rnelson/asail/guide/guide.html

New perspectives on the West: William F. Cody. (2001). Retrieved October 10, 2013, from http://www.pbs.org/weta/thewest/people/a_c/buffalobill.htm

Olivas, M. A. (1996). Indian, Chicano, and Puerto Rican colleges: Status and issues. In C. Turner, M. Garcia, A. Nora, & L. I. Rendón (Eds.), *Racial and ethnic diversity in higher education*. Boston, MA: Pearson Custom Publishing.

Owen, M., & Maurer, K. (2012). *No easy day: The firsthand account of the mission that killed Osama Bin Laden*. New York, NY: Dutton.

Pewewardy, C., & Frey, B. (2004). American Indian students' perceptions of racial climate, multicultural support services, and ethnic fraud at a predominantly White university. *Journal of American Indian Education, 43*(1), 32–60.

Project MALES: Mentoring to Achieve Latino Educational Success. (n.d.). Retrieved October 10, 2013, from http://ddce.utexas.edu/projectmales/

Public school graduates and dropouts from the common core of data: School year 2007–08. (2010). Retrieved October 17, 2013, from nces.ed.gov/pubs2010/2010341.pdf

Ramirez, R. K. (2009). Henry Roe Cloud: A granddaughter's Native feminist biographical account. *Wicazo Sa Review, 24*(2), 77–103.

Rindone, P. (1988). Achievement motivation and academic achievement of Native American students. *Journal of American Indian Education, 28*(1), 1–8.

Ross, L. (2009). From the "F" word to indigenous/feminisms. *Wicazo Sa Review, 24*(2), 39–52.

Ross, T., Kena, G., Rathbun, A., KewalRamani, A., Zhang, J., Kristapovich, P., & Manning, E. (2012). *Higher education: Gaps in access and persistence study* (NCES 2012-046). Washington, DC: Government Printing Office.

Schwarz, M. T. (1997). *Molded in the image of changing woman: Navajo views on the human body and personhood.* Tucson: University of Arizona Press.

Simpson, A. (2009). Captivating Eunice: Membership, colonialism, and gendered citizenships of grief. *Wicazo Sa Review, 24*(2), 105–129.

Sitting Bull. (2013). Retrieved October 10, 2013, from http://www.sittingbull.org/

Smith, P. C., & Warrior, R. A. (1996). *Like a hurricane: The Indian movement from Alcatraz to Wounded Knee.* New York, NY: New Press.

Snyder, T. D., & Dillow, S. A. (2012). *Digest of education statistics 2011* (NCES 2012-001). Washington, DC: National Center for Education Statistics, Institute of Education Sciences, U.S. Department of Education. Retrieved October 17, 2013, from http://nces.ed.gov/pubs2012/2012001.pdf

Spring, J. (2009). *Deculturalization and the struggle for equality: A brief history of the education of dominated cultures in the United States* (6th ed.). Boston, MA: McGraw-Hill.

Stillwell, R. (2010). *Public school graduates and dropouts from the common core of data: School year 2007–08 (NCES 2010-341).* Washington, DC: National Center for Education Statistics, Institute of Education Sciences, U.S. Department of Education. Retrieved December 11, 2012, from http://nces.ed.gov.pubsearch/pubsinfo .asp?pubid=2010341

Suina, S. E. (1987). *The American Indian drop-out problem: A look at Pueblo Indian freshmen, sophomores, and juniors in six colleges and universities in New Mexico* (Unpublished doctoral dissertation). Pennsylvania State University, University Park.

Takaki, R. (1993). *A different mirror: A history of multicultural America.* Boston, MA: Little, Brown.

TallBear, K. (2013). *Indigeneity and technoscience: About Kim TallBear.* Retrieved October 10, 2013, from http://www.kimtallbear.com/about.html

Torres, V., & Bitsói, L. (2011). American Indian college students. In M. J. Cuyjet, M. F. Howard-Hamilton, & D. L. Cooper (Eds.), *Multiculturalism on campus: Theories, models, and practices for understanding diversity and creating inclusion* (pp. 169–189). Sterling, VA: Stylus.

Waziyatawin, A. W. (2003, Winter/Spring). Decolonizing the 1862 death marches. *American Indian Quarterly, 28*, 185–215.

Welcome to call me MISTER. (2013). Retrieved October 10, 2013, from http://www .clemson.edu/hehd/departments/education/research/callmemister/

Wildcat, D. R. (2001). The question of self-determination. In V. Deloria, Jr. & D. R. Wildcat (Eds.), *Power and place: Indian education in America* (pp. 135–150). Golden, CO: Fulcrum Resources.

Wright, B. (1988). "For the children of the infidels?": American Indian education in the colonial colleges. *American Indian Culture and Research Journal, 12*(3), 1–14.

4

MASCULINITY

Through a Latino Male Lens

Victor B. Sáenz and Beth E. Bukoski

The male education crisis narrative has grown louder among the mainstream media in recent years, and it has been embodied by the faces of White boys (e.g., see Tyre, 2006; Wilson, 2007). This recognition of the challenges young men confront as they navigate the educational pipeline is an example of how White middle-class heteronormative patriarchy has structured our understanding of the problem of boys. White boys represent the face of the crisis and have served to legitimize it in the mainstream, yet boys and men of color remain the specter in the shadows—an invisible threat silently lurking and representing the way patriarchy structures boys' lives in detrimental ways.

In the Latino population, for example, the educational attainment gap between Latino males and their female peers has been widening since the 1970s. As of 2010 Latino males obtained 38.4 percent of all associate's and bachelor's degrees awarded to Latinos (Ennis, Rios-Vargas, & Albert, 2011), and this gap is only projected to increase (Sáenz & Ponjuan, 2011). Even as the number of Latinas/Latinos attending college and attaining degrees has increased steadily over the last few decades, the proportional representation of Latino males continues to decline relative to their female peers (Sáenz & Ponjuan, 2009). The growing Latino gender gap—a trend also evident in other racial/ethnic groups—has untold implications for public policy and educational practice, as Latino males are more likely than their female counterparts to drop out of high school, to join the workforce rather than attend college, or to leave college before graduating (Sáenz & Ponjuan, 2009).

This is not to suggest that the long-term success of female students has been ensured or that it has come at the expense of male students, as structural and gender inequalities remain pervasive in American society. Nonetheless, when we conjoin the growing gender gap with the persistent educational attainment gap between Latinas and Latinos and other racial and ethnic groups in this country, the sobering reality facing Latino males is cause for concern. The dual questions of why Latino males are losing ground in accessing higher education and what it could portend over time for this community are at the heart of this chapter. Indeed, we believe researchers and higher education practitioners must reenvision the study of Latino college-age males and all men of color entirely and consider methods and tools that not only name but also deconstruct gender differences in educational outcomes.

Little research exists that provides a meaningful precedence for how to study Latino men (or men in general) as gendered beings. In the field of higher education, the work is still limited in scope and depth but helps to demonstrate the dearth of methods available for studying men as men. Men in postsecondary contexts have been studied across multiple domains—identity development, gender socialization, sexuality and sexual orientation, destructive behaviors, wellness issues, spirituality, and sports (Harper, Carini, Bridges, & Hayek, 2004; Harper & Harris, 2010; Harris & Martin, 2006). In their study of men on community college campuses, for example, Harris and Harper (2008) used O'Neil's (1981) male gender role conflict (MGRC) as an analytical framework and found all participants experienced MGRC. In addition, although there are frameworks for understanding Latino identity development (e.g., Ferdman & Gallegos, 2001), no research to date explores men's gendered identity development; rather, identity development models were based on men, but naturalized gender did not consider men as gendered beings (Meth & Pasick, 1990), which led to an overreliance on gender stereotypes (Davis, 2010).

These examples illustrate our point aptly: The only models available to researchers are outdated, limited in applicability, or have yet to be created. Much of what we know about men in college, therefore, focuses on men as a group without considering men as gendered beings. In other words, gender is a taken-for-granted construct, naturalized through its invisibility, and used organizationally and categorically rather than as a socially constructed phenomenon. Some studies (e.g., Josselson & Harway, 2012; Kaufman, 1999; Richmond, Levant, & Ladhani, 2012) suggest that intersectionality can be used to understand men in more nuanced ways, and Kimmel (2008) begins to describe the social mechanisms that maintain these masculine norms. Nonetheless, we are left with few analytical tools to use in understanding Latino males and men of color in new ways, especially during their formative college years.

Therefore, we suggest in this chapter that we must change how we look at men of color in college by appropriating feminist methods, which have already proven immensely useful in deconstructing gender and patriarchy. We do so by illustrating how we can deploy feminist approaches in the study of Latino males in college. To develop this argument further, however, we need to step back and understand the contributions of the feminist movement(s) and the masculinist movement to put their contributions in perspective and find a way forward. The chapter concludes with implications for practice as well as an exploration of a new model for Latino male mentoring.

A New Approach—Patriarchy and Feminist Methods

We suggest that contemporary trends in research have to do with the way male gender has come to be naturalized even within scholarly realms. We believe researchers and professionals must move beyond naming and describing hegemonic masculinity and consider adopting feminist methods, which seek to actively disrupt White middle-class heteronormative patriarchy and work toward changing social attitudes. Indeed, research on men in higher education (e.g., Harper & Harris, 2010; Kimmel & Davis, 2011; Wagner, 2011) also claims that feminist methods need to be leveraged to aid in the study of men. And findings by the College Board (2011) suggest that men of color in particular could be well served by this empirical borrowing, considering that based on their unique social positions, they access power differently.

Latino males and other men of color in college face a different kind of problem than their White peers because their socialization is not only gendered but also raced. As Gordon and Henery discuss in Chapter 1, men of color seek Respectability and Reputation in public and private spheres. The degree to which a young man is able to access the social, cultural, and financial capital needed to gain Respectability often is manifested in stark choices not unlike the choices once (and, in some ways, still) constricting women's lives. Men of color often must choose between legal Respectability with confinement to a low-paying, often dead-end job, or illegal Respectability with financial freedom but ultimately with the possibility of imprisonment because of criminal activity. For some men of color, a third option is a door that leads to education; social mobility; redefinitions of manhood on personal terms; and social, personal, and economic success. But this third option is invisible and unknown except as an abstract idea to many young men.

We see the manifestation of patriarchy's influence on Latino men in predominant stereotypes as well, which helps to illustrate the way gender, race, and class mutually constitute each other to structure men's lives. A quick search on Google of the phrase "stereotype Hispanic or Latino" yielded several terms the reader will no doubt find familiar—*wetback*, or the idea that all Latinos are illegal immigrants; *lazy worker*, implying that Latinos do not work hard; *domestic*, suggesting Latinos all work in menial jobs as domestics or field or landscape workers; *lover*, casting Latinos as hypersexual; *Spanish-speaking Latino*, indicating all Latinos do not speak and have no interest in learning English; and *Latin Kings*, implying that many Latinos choose gangs and crime instead of lives as productive citizens. All of these stereotypes tap into forms of White middle-class heteronormative patriarchy in some way, either by buying into part of the construction of patriarchy (hypersexuality) or by resisting that patriarchy in nonproductive or destructive ways (gangsterism).

For men of color, ascribing to and resisting patriarchy are prisons of masculinity, with White middle-class heteronormative values standing guard, limiting options and choices, and denying men even the ability to name what is shaping their lives. Feminists helped women to name sexism and the negative influence of patriarchy on women's lives (Freedman, 2002), and feminism also has tools to help us name and deconstruct patriarchy and its negative influence on men's lives. By giving us a vocabulary and the scholarly tools to name and deconstruct patriarchy, feminism could help men in the way it helped women break through female stereotypes, redefine womanhood, and expand options. Furthermore, if men of color become able to name and understand how patriarchy is shaping their lives, they will become allies in the work still needing to be done on feminist fronts (e.g., the persistent wage gap, domestic violence, reproductive rights).

Feminism has given us the rhetoric to understand and frame patriarchy in constructive ways and has given us tools to use in deconstructing gender in explicit ways. Black feminists and Chicana feminists, in particular, have developed a language to understand the simultaneous presence of privilege and disprivilege in their lives and, hence, our own lives. Despite the plethora of tools that would help us to deconstruct White middle-class heteronormative patriarchy's influence on young men of color, however, research to date has instead largely served to reify gender and, as Gordon and Henery illustrate in Chapter 1, has used an implicit deficit and patriarchal framing to do so. There is, therefore, a need for a radical change in the way we talk about Latino males and other young men of color and a reconceptualization of how we study them.

Mapping Feminism and Masculism

Feminist tools reexamine how patriarchy affects men of color because feminism questions the status quo and takes into account the absence of a neutral patriarchal norm. We have much to catch up on, though, since women's equity has been on our social and political agendas for over 100 years. The feminist movement employed myriad methods and stratagems to gain rights, expand access, and move toward equity across various domains, including domestic violence, women's health, workplace equity, and expanding access for women in historically male-dominated professions (Freedman, 2002). The efforts of feminists and their allies have had an unrelenting focus on women as gendered beings who must operate inside a gendered social system. These efforts have served to transform women's professional and personal landscapes.

The same cannot be said for the men's movement—a tenuous phrase, to say the least, and much less in the public eye. There has been a focus on men since the 1970s, particularly in psychology (e.g., O'Neil, 1981), but men's equity has remained largely absent from public discourse until the past decade when mainstream articles and books began to focus on ideas such as *the missing men, fall of masculinity, the war against boys,* and *the decline of men* (e.g., Sommers, 2000; Tyre, 2006). These provocative pieces did help to spur men's studies, though, and we now have more information to contextualize the study of men in the 21st century.

In addition, work on the college experiences of Latino males and men of color (e.g., College Board, 2011) indicates that they experience one or more areas of conflict, such as in family expectations, self-perception, image, and balancing multiple responsibilities. This begins to echo what we know about how women negotiate the second shift at home, encounter the glass ceiling at work, and negotiate multiple roles attached to their gender. Indeed, we would not know as much as we do about women's lives if it were not for the efforts of the feminist movement in seeking to understand women's lived experiences, contributions, and the systemic barriers they face. Similarly, we would not know as much as we do about the experiences of women of color were it not for the theoretical advances provided by Black feminists and Chicana feminists who sought to expand our understanding of the role of intersections of gender and race in structuring the lives of women. If the women's movement yielded myriad positive effects for women, it is reasonable to consider how these methods could yield positive outcomes for men. It is also reasonable to consider how Chicana feminist thought can serve as a useful lens to critically examine the experiences of Latino males in college.

A Brief Overview of the Women's Movement: A Focus on Chicana Feminism

Until a century ago, women in the United States were considered property and were denied citizenship, voice, and participation because of their perceived delicate natures and the inherent weakness of their sex (Freedman, 2002). The first wave of feminist thought began to dispel socially perpetuated myths by focusing on women's gaining fundamental rights long foreclosed. In the 19th and early 20th centuries, feminists focused on equal rights in contracts, marriage, parenting, and property. By the end of the 19th century, there was also a focus on political power, particularly through voting rights, best illustrated through the pioneering work of Elizabeth Cady Stanton, Susan B. Anthony, and documents such as the Declaration of Sentiments at Seneca Falls in 1848 (see Schneir, 1994). These efforts led to the enactment of the 19th Amendment in 1920 and, through continued legal and political reform, began chipping away at inequalities in marriage, contract, and property rights, and began reforming basic employment laws that put women at a disadvantage.

The second wave of feminism gained momentum in the 1960s with a perspective influenced by Marxism and existentialism, and focused on a wider range of equity issues such as sexuality, reproductive rights, de facto inequalities, and discrimination. This wave of activist feminists and their allies yielded changes in rape, custody, and divorce laws as well as the creation of battered women's centers and a partial closing of the wage gap. Works that help illustrate this period include Simone de Beauvoir's (1949/2011) *The Second Sex*, Betty Friedan's (1964) *The Feminine Mystique*, and the legal efforts of Supreme Court justice Ruth Bader Ginsburg. A key contribution of second wave feminism, which gave rise to Chicana feminism and Black feminism, was a language that named patriarchy and sexism and their effects on women, tools that Chicana feminists and Black feminists carried forward into even more nuanced ways of understanding and describing White middle-class heteronormative patriarchy's influence.

The third wave of feminism, which partially overlaps the second wave, reflects a schism with differences of opinion concerning how women could best be served regarding pornography and sexuality. For instance, there is a focus on sexual liberation, with one camp viewing prostitutes as active agents in their own lives and maintaining control through stipulating services and fees. From this perspective, prostitutes are considered sexually liberated and may enjoy their work (e.g., see the work of Gayle Rubin, 2011; see Freedman, 2002, for a more in-depth discussion of the history of feminism).

Just as all political and social movements have weaknesses, so does the Feminist movement. In its incipient years, feminism was often racially noninclusive from fear of losing traction with White male political alliances. There have been debates over the place of lesbians and transwomen in the feminist discussion as well as disagreement over the aims to be achieved (particularly in the third wave), and disagreements over how to achieve shared aims, for example, Ginsburg's contested methods of litigating on behalf of men to push forward equality goals (see Campbell, 2004).

Even with its weaknesses and the still evolving nature of feminism in contemporary society, the examination of women as gendered beings has had far-reaching, positive effects on women and girls through multiple domains. These strides for women and girls were accomplished on the shoulders of feminists who employed multiple strategies related to policy and law, theory, and even biology and chemistry. It is also important to remember that gaps and policy issues persist concerning equity, particularly in areas such as violence against women, third world feminism, and women's reproductive rights, which are still highly contested domains.

Feminist Methods

Regardless of the gender equity battles still raging and those yet to be fought, an emerging arsenal of techniques has allowed feminists and feminist allies to continue to push the equity agenda forward in positive ways. Feminist efforts, therefore, have resulted in a real-world impact on the lives of women by expanding research on biology, sex, and gender; providing a platform and language to create and support women's rights movements in international and third world settings; raising awareness of, and money for, women's health issues; creating and sustaining women's and gender studies departments and centers; creating dialogue with, and spaces for, allied work with lesbian, gay, bisexual, transgender, and queer or questioning communities; expanding theoretical perspectives to consider gender in multiple ways; and expanding access to previously male-dominated domains, including politics, sports, business, and—critically—education.

Those focusing on men in higher education and in wider political and social realms, therefore, could learn and benefit from these strides, borrowing from legal theories, identity development models, materiality studies, feminist standpoint theory, queer theory, and gender performative theory (we briefly touch on each of these later in this section). Indeed, feminist methods and their social and political impact provide quite a precedent that could prove to be a new driving force in the discussion and study of men, particularly in light of the inadequacies of existing work devoted to them.

Researchers and professionals may want to consider several methodological tools in their work with young men of color (see Olesen, 2011, for a more thorough discussion of 21st-century qualitative feminist research). Feminist legal methods (Bartlett & Rhode, 2009), for instance, provide fodder for analysis. Formal equality, which focuses on whether men and women receive equal treatment (punishment, resources, etc.), could inform our understanding of how young men gain access to educational resources and whether young men are receiving equal treatment. Nonsubordination theory, by focusing on sex-based domination, could explore whether educational policies serve to subordinate men and women in unique ways. This perspective would help higher education faculty and students alike to begin to recognize that systems can privilege and disprivilege men and women in unique ways; this perspective also helps to deconstruct claims that laws and policies naturalize men as powerful and women as powerless, particularly through issues such as sexual harassment, pornography, domestic violence, and heterosexuality.

Difference theory (Bartlett & Rhode, 2009), which views some gender differences not as barriers to overcome but as potentially valuable resources that provide a better model for legal and social institutions, could help men see the value in some feminine behaviors and would help to continue to deconstruct gender stereotypes. Autonomy theory (Bartlett & Rhode, 2009) would shift the focus from men reaching for idealized and hegemonic masculine ideals to men searching for autonomy and fulfillment unfettered by a need to conform to masculine ideals. And, as has been mentioned, focusing on multiple aspects of identity and the way they interact to amplify, mute, or transform one's experience with law, policy, and institutions, thus encompassing masculinity as privilege and disprivilege, would help researchers and policymakers move away from female gender as the sole focus of their efforts. In addition, intersectionality resists notions of identity politics and biological notions of male and female categories.

Another feminist perspective that could aid in the study of men is materialism. Materialism grew from Marxist capitalism, which sees dismantling capitalism as a way of liberating women, and explicitly examines the distribution of inequities of resources, knowledge, and power (Hennessy & Ingraham, 1997). From this perspective, ownership of private property is a mechanism that maintains patriarchy and social inequality. Materialism, in particular, illustrates the finding we explicate later in the chapter regarding Latino males' interest in financial success and studies that show class and gender intersect meaningfully for men from lower socioeconomic backgrounds. Examining men's lives through their material possessions, spaces, and objects, actualized and desired, would provide valuable insight into the way masculinity is constructed, enacted, and resisted.

A feminist standpoint is another valuable tool (Harding, 2008). Feminist standpoint theory seeks to understand the dynamics of power and oppression by examining how dominant groups maintain privilege as well as how oppressed groups gain leverage and change dominant systems (Wood, 2011). Standpoint theory recognizes that an individual may claim membership in multiple groups and that these memberships shape individualized perspectives, including how individuals make sense of their social worlds and subjective experiences (Wood, 2011). Standpoint theory subscribes to several key ideas: Power dynamics are perceived quite differently depending on a person's social location, no single right perspective exists, what people do influences their perspective (e.g., knowledge, consciousness, identity), and every standpoint is partial and limited in some way. There is a difference, though, between social location and standpoint.

Standpoint does not intrinsically flow from location but is developed through individual critical reflection of power dynamics and construction of an oppositional stance (Wood, 2011). For example, people in more privileged positions may have a distorted view of those without privilege, in part because such distortion is necessary to maintaining power. A feminist standpoint, which is particularly relevant to issues of gender, can arise from being female, but this is not necessarily the case. When applied to men, standpoint could be quite powerful. How do men come to take a stance in opposition to hegemonic masculinity? What processes do men experience that help them productively resist hegemonic masculinity and find ways to perform masculinity in productive, socially responsible ways?

Another theory that may be of use is queer theory (Sullivan, 2003). Queer theory critiques conventional categories of identity and cultural values of "normal" and "abnormal," particularly in relation to sexuality. Proponents of this theory argue that identities are not fixed but rather somewhat fluid. Queer theory does not only pertain to lesbian, gay, bisexual, trans, and queer communities, however; it can be applied to any departure from what society deems as being normal. Normative masculinity has potentially negative effects on men (Mahalik, Englar-Carlson, & Good, 2003), making it worth exploring how men make nonnormative choices and perform gender in nontraditional ways.

Gender performance could also make substantive contributions to the study of men as men. One key notion of performative theory holds that gender comes into being only through expression and performance; thus, seen in this way, *gender* is not a noun but a verb, an act of doing, becoming, and living (Denzin, 2003). And, although gender is performed, it is performed in myriad ways, conventional and unconventional. A second key notion is that our performances of gender are not one-person shows; they are collaborative and draw on social meanings that transcend our individual experiences. In other words, we are culturally coded with stylized performances of gender, and who, where, and why we're interacting with someone or more than one person (physically or mentally) influences us in different contexts and at different times (Wood, 2011). Performative theory can help us understand, for instance, how men perform the strong-and-silent construction of masculinity; how Latino men perform machismo; and, more broadly, how men perform maleness in school contexts as well as how social contexts encourage particular kinds of performances.

Finally, queer performance theory merges queer theory and performance theory by examining performances that are other than those deemed normal by society, those that challenge and destabilize cultural categories and values (Wood, 2011). Of particular interest are queer performances that are everyday and routine. In this way, queer performances can become political tools that unsettle normalized or naturalized social structures and ideologies (Butler, 1993, 2004). Using queer performative theory could aid in understanding how men make choices about their nontraditional gender performances and how these choices influence the educational context by resisting socially acceptable masculine norms.

Feminist methods could be of huge benefit to studying all men of color. For example, standpoint theory could help us understand the role of ritual and traditions in the formation of the male standpoint among Native American men, performative theory could inform our understanding of how Asian American men negotiate dominant social discourses that argue Asian men are sexless by examining how men perform masculinity, and materiality could explore the role of possessions and wealth in African American men's gender performance. These are merely a few examples of the kind of study needed regarding men in higher education.

Furthermore, research pioneered by feminist scholars of color that seeks to endarken epistemic stances (Dillard & Okpalaoka, 2011), decolonize methods (Anzaldúa, 1987), and protect Indigenous knowledge (Battiste, 2008) may seem radical but also is potentially fruitful to consider. Such is the case with Black feminism and Chicana feminism, which we discuss further in the next section.

Black and Chicana Feminism

Two more critical contributions of feminists to the way we are reframing the study of men are Black and Chicana feminism. Black feminism can be traced to the first women's antislavery movement society formed in 1832 and the account of Sojourner Truth's speech in 1851 at the Women's Rights Convention in which she questioned major truth claims of the patriarchal slave system by asking, "And ain't I a woman?" (Brah & Phoenix, 2004, p. 76). Black feminist thought also has roots in the civil rights era and the work of luminaries such as W. E. B. Du Bois and Maria Stewart, who "claimed the right to articulate a sense of self and act on it" (Dill & Zambrana, 2009, p. 3). This legacy of recognizing and articulating ways of knowing other than the normative White male Eurocentric vision still common to the 19th century represents a departure in understanding power relations, knowledge claims, and the construction of society.

Another historic touchstone is the political project known as the Combahee River Collective. In 1977 this Black lesbian feminist organization rejected the notion of privileging any single aspect of identity over another. In a well-known statement, members instead embraced an "integrated analysis and practice based upon the fact that the major systems of oppression are interlocking" (Combahee River Collective, 1981, p. 210). A key contribution of Black feminist thought is intersectionality, which is concerned with validating and articulating a sense of self through multiple, interlocking categories of difference (e.g., race, class, and gender; Cole, 2009; Collins, 2000; Crenshaw, 1991; hooks, 2000). The utility of intersectionality in the study of young men of color is further explored with regard to Asian American and Pacific Islander men in Chapter 2 of this book.

Chicana feminist education scholars also have pushed our notions of social inquiry by encouraging us to move beyond hegemonic categories of scholarship and instead embrace a "decolonization" of the research process through a Chicana feminist lens (Calderón Delgado Bernal, Pérez Huber, Malagón, & Nelly Vélez, 2012). For example, Elenes (2011) notes that the process of decolonizing frameworks of analysis is aimed at reclaiming neglected voices and discovering new insights that would otherwise be unavailable or invisible. Chicana scholars draw on their ways of knowing to disrupt hegemonic categories of analysis, create decolonizing methodologies, and expand our understanding of what it means to employ a Chicana feminist lens (Calderón et al., 2012). In short, the last 20 years of work in Chicana feminist frameworks has contributed unique and important insights as well as made valuable contributions to theory, methodology, and pedagogy in education. It is in this spirit that we propose using such a lens to examine the experience of Latino males.

It is unprecedented and perhaps provocative to propose using a Chicana feminist framework to study the experiences of Latino males in college. No doubt critics will claim it is unproductive to do so, yet the very antihegemonic nature of feminist inquiry rejects the notion of fixed rules. Our contention is that an application of a Chicana feminist framework will allow us to derive unique and emergent findings and insights that have otherwise been unavailable within our existing research on Latino males. We recognize the risk inherent in proposing the use of feminism in men's studies; however, we hope that by opening ourselves to critique, we also open ourselves to a conversation, a conversation we welcome. Before turning to an application of Chicana feminism to research, however, we briefly delineate the evolution of the men's movement.

Men's Movement: A Brief(er) Overview

The men's movement began in the 1970s, in part as a reaction to or reapplication of the women's movement (Lewis, 1981). Men began examining masculinity and becoming more reflective about the negative consequences of some forms of masculinity. Issues that served to coalesce the movement include reproductive rights, divorce laws, domestic violence laws, and sexual harassment laws. The fathers' rights movement also gained momentum in the late 1970s. For example, the National Coalition for Men was founded in 1977 and is the oldest men's group committed to ending sex discrimination against men (Crouch, 2011). In addition, the terms *masculism* and *masculinism* gained some traction in the 1990s, particularly on issues such as violence, parenting, discrimination, social issues, education, and employment (Cree & Cavanagh, 1996).

While there is no clear road map of the development of men's studies, we highlight here some of the key research that has informed our current stance regarding the use of feminism in the study of men.[1] Two major contributions to the field are the work of Raewyn Connell (1995) and Christina Hoff Sommers (2000). A transwoman, Connell has produced work that centers on the social construction of masculinity. She covers a variety of topics from archetypes to men's bodies to contemporary politics. Sommers is a self-described "equity feminist" who faults contemporary feminism for "its irrational hostility to men, its recklessness with facts and statistics, and its inability to take seriously the possibility that the sexes are equal—but different" (Sommers, 2000, pp. 18–19). In addition, contemporary discourse seems to be working toward an understanding of the paradoxical nature of masculinity. For example, contemporary work (e.g., Pollack, 1999) highlights how boyhood is often an *emotional wasteland*, and although men have power, they often feel powerless. In other words, we are working toward a notion, as intersectionality claims, that men are privileged and disprivileged simultaneously (Richmond et al., 2012).

Theoretical insights concerning masculinity have largely focused on the way socially constructed masculinities are psychosocially detrimental. Brannon (1976), for example, delineated four fundamental rules of masculinity that hold that masculinity entails consistent rejection of femininity (no sissy stuff); measuring self-worth on power, status, and wealth (the big wheel); being stoic and highly rational in crises (the sturdy oak); and taking risks through daring and aggressive behavior (give 'em hell). O'Neil (1981) took this idea a step further and argued that "men's gender role socialization and the values of the masculine mystique produce a devaluation of feminine values and a learned fear of femininity" (p. 203). Gender role socialization, then, manifests itself in six patterns of gender role conflict and strain: restrictive emotionality; socialized control, power, and competition issues;

homophobia; restrictive sexual and affectionate behavior; obsession with achievement and success; and health care problems (O'Neil, 1981).

Research on men as men has also focused on adolescence and the socialization process, again largely focusing on the detrimental impact of heteronormative notions of masculinity. The boy code (Pollack, 1999; Pollack & Shuster, 2001), for example, specifies that boys are socially compelled to act tough, not admit emotionality, and dismiss the pain of others and themselves. Reiterating these psychological masculine norms and their detrimental impact, Mahalik et al. (2003) describe "masculine scripting" used by men in psychotherapy. While producing positive effects such as men feeling empowered at work or home through competition, these scripts also proved quite detrimental to men, resulting in psychological distress, trouble with the law, and violence against women. Commonly cited scripts include strong and silent, tough guy, "give 'em hell," playboy, homophobic, winner, and independent. This body of psychologically focused work has given us ways to name and identify detrimental masculine ideologies or the effect of patriarchy on men's lives; however, it has done little to probe the boundaries of patriarchy, to understand multiple or intersectional ways of *doing* masculinity, or to deconstruct the systems that sustain patriarchy.

From a sociological standpoint, Kimmel (2008) mapped "Guyland," a realm where boys encounter a collection of attitudes, values, and characteristics that constitute what it means to be a man, including boys don't cry; it's better to be mad than sad; don't get mad, get even; take it like a man; he who has the most toys when he dies wins; just do it, or ride or die; size matters; I don't stop to ask for directions; nice guys finish last; and it's all good. Kimmel further argues that three cultures socialize young men and serve to perpetuate rigid, normative constructions of masculinity. The culture of entitlement allows privilege and superiority to be naturalized and decreases the ability of young men to empathize with others. The culture of silence requires that boys suffer pain and cruelty by themselves and become complicit in the suffering of others, all borne in silence. Finally, the culture of protection dismisses bad behavior and contributes to antisocial and excessive behaviors. Kimmel notes these cultures are not maintained solely by men in America; they are also sustained by families, communities, institutions, and loved ones, in part because they so often remain unquestioned.

In an important theoretical move forward, Richmond et al. (2012) argue for the use of more intersectional analysis of men's experiences because of the way men access power and privilege differently based on their intersectional identities (i.e., a Brown man and a White man access power differently, as do a poor man and a rich man, a heterosexual and a homosexual—to point out a few identities that intersect meaningfully with gender). Josselson and Harway (2012) also argue that stereotyping men as a monolithic group through masculine homogeneity masks nuances of race and sexual relations within the male experience. These movements away from monolithic and heteronormative notions of masculinity mark an important shift toward moving beyond naming masculinity; however, this work could move further and faster if proven tools (i.e., feminism) were used.

Work on men as men, therefore, has been under way since the 1970s and, particularly in psychology and clinical psychology, has received a good deal of attention. However, while the reader most likely at least recognizes the names of Elizabeth Cady Stanton and Betty Friedan, it is doubtful the reader has heard of many, if any, of the names previously mentioned. And, despite this base of work on men as gendered beings, there is still a dearth of theoretical or conceptual tools available to study men as men. Furthermore, most of the work on men as gendered beings is serving to reify gender socialization as destructive. This claim, however, must be pushed further to explore how socialization takes place, how men are able to adapt successfully to socialization pressure, and how social institutions such as schools can help men navigate these processes productively instead of destructively.

While current male-focused research aptly names and labels gendered constructions, they are too rigid and hegemonic to account for the fluidity of gender and do little to aid in understanding the construction of masculinity or to deconstruct the influence of patriarchy. Indeed, as Gordon and Henery illustrate in Chapter 1, the work surrounding men of color is not only lacking in theory, it is often implicitly employing a deficit theory. Later research, such as that by Richmond et al. (2012), is beginning to use some explicitly feminist methods such as intersectionality to explore men's lives; however, this is just the beginning of what feminist thought and methods could lend to the study of men of color.

Feminist Methods in the Study of Latino Males

To demonstrate the latent potential of feminism in the study of men of color, we turn specifically to Latino males in college as a subgroup. As mentioned previously, rates of educational attainment among Latino males are diminishing (Sáenz & Ponjuan, 2009, 2011). When one considers the growing Latino population, it is difficult not to conclude that this situation will have an economic, social, and political impact if left to continue on its current trajectory. There is a growing focus on Latino males, however, and we draw from those who have preceded us in developing our work.

For example, research exists that relates specifically to conceptions of masculinity within Latino subgroups. Research constructs of Latino masculinity focus on machismo and *caballerismo*. Machismo refers to characteristics largely in line with masculinity constructs already mentioned, such as assertiveness, power, control, aggression, and obsession with achieving status (e.g., see De La Cancela, 1993; Rodriguez & Gonzales, 1997; Torres, Solberg, & Carlstrom, 2002). Caballerismo, partly in reaction to the negative connotations of machismo, focuses on positive instantiations of masculinity such as chivalrousness, family centeredness, nurturing stances, and approaching of problems from a more emotionally connected perspective (Arciniega, Anderson, Tovar-Blank, & Tracey, 2008).

Some of the more contemporary works on Latino men, therefore, are moving away from deficit orientations and toward more positive dispositions. For example, we can see the effects of White middle-class heteronormative patriarchy in studies (e.g., Mirandé, 1997) that found that masculine hegemonic attributes are often seen as positive, connoting strength, virility, and sex appeal when attached to White/European figures and celebrities, and connoting negative characteristics when attached to men of color. There is also research examining the intersection of race and class and their simultaneous influence on men's ability to access social and financial capital; when young men are denied access, they often revert to nonproductive resistance stances or hypermasculinity (e.g., De La Cancela, 1981; Ramírez, 1999; Torres et al., 2002). These studies are largely descriptive but represent an important breakthrough in beginning to deconstruct notions of masculinity for males of color.

Rethinking the Latino Male Research Agenda

We seek here not only to push forward our own research on Latino males but also to provide a tangible example for how feminist methods can be used productively to reframe the gender equity agenda. In this section we provide some of our thematic findings from a study of Latino males at community colleges in Texas (Sáenz, Bukoski, Lu, & Rodriguez, 2012) and use quotations from data collected for that study in focus groups at community colleges in Texas. This analysis used MGRC, supplemented by constructs of machismo and caballerismo. We should note that researchers (Harper & Harris, 2010) have provided a precedent for using MGRC to study men of color in community colleges. In the following section we reexamine a segment of data using a Chicana feminist perspective to illustrate the potential of employing feminist methods in the study of men. The findings and initial analysis were drawn from a qualitative study conducted at five community colleges in Texas (Sáenz et al., 2012). We delineate the following two major findings—the complex influence of pride and the resistance to help-seeking behaviors—which we have also begun to explore in ongoing scholarly papers (e.g., Sáenz et al., 2012).

Complex Influence of Pride

Traditional concepts of masculinity emphasize the importance of remaining tough, or strong and silent, in the face of challenges and avoiding displays of emotion, which can be perceived as a weakness or as overly feminine (or sissy). For male college students, this can translate into avoiding asking for help, even in the face of imminent failure (Gloria, Castellanos, Scull, & Villegas, 2009; Sáenz & Ponjuan, 2009). Students often labeled their resistance to seeking help as pride or machismo.

It is important to note the paradox in this concept. On the one hand, men's pride, or machismo, is a source of strength, propelling them to achieve more and work harder for their goals, as one young man from our study's data stated:

> I was in, uh, ROTC. Junior reserve officer training corps, at my high school. And they're pretty much . . . they taught me how to be a leader. How to take responsibility, to take charge when nobody else is doing nothing about it, and that's pretty much how I became prepared to come over here. Because, at home, well, I don't want to say they don't support me, it's just that they just can't because, because if I ask for help . . . well I'm the first in my family to graduate from college; I'm sorry to graduate from high school and to attend college. So, uh, I'm pretty much the first doing everything. It's just me, myself, and I at home, so . . .

This student sees his educational pathway as being forged by "me, myself, and I" and attributes to the military—a systematic indoctrination of the masculine ideals of strength, silence, and toughness—the role of proving ground for his sense of masculinity. This student's sense of pride, therefore, is attached to his identity as a man and his identity as the first in his family to graduate from high school. Both are key driving forces in his achievement. They also create a large burden he feels is unshareable with his family. They cannot understand, and so his masculine ideal and his sense of pride drive him to further isolation.

On the other hand, pride/machismo could have negative consequences that men were cognizant of. Men directly stated that they knew machismo was a barrier to their academic success:

> It think it's because, uh, well, well maybe it's because of machismo, a guy, he wants to be a man, and he wants to get a job, like right away to impress women. So, therefore, they do all these things to support their family, and because a wife doesn't want to be a housewife anymore, they try to, I don't know, go to work or something, but because a man is a macho, so they send the woman to college instead. Well, at least this is from my friends, because

my friends, they don't, my male friends, they don't go to college, but their wives do. And this is what I've seen, because my male friends, they do want to support their family, and they want to send their wives to college.

This student reveals an unspoken code of Latino masculinity: Education is not macho enough for Latino males to attain education and status as a male in the community. Wives, therefore, and (unspoken) daughters go to college, but macho men do not. In addition, the ability to get a job and by extension to have money become ways to achieve masculine status, in part through impressing women.

The concept of pride/machismo, therefore, is positive and negative. Machismo can have a negative connotation, indicating hypermasculinity. At the same time, machismo is a term commonly used to describe Latino men culturally and societally. As a result, many young Latino men fall victim to a self-fulfilling prophecy; they internalize societal expectations in negative ways, staying tough even when it is to their detriment developmentally and educationally. This phenomenon manifested itself when they were asked why they do not seek help or why they do not admit a lack of comprehension of material. Rather than answering the question directly, many young men place blame on machismo and respond that they are just "too proud," "too stubborn," or "too dismissive" to pursue a college education or even use institutional resources. Pride/machismo was also a source of strength, however, propelling men to achieve and work harder for success.

Fear and Pride Inhibit Help-Seeking Behaviors

The notion of pride was often expressed in conjunction with feelings of fear. Men indicated that despite their overt pride and confidence, they were often afraid of failing. This fear manifested itself as anxiety and a perception of education as yielding high-stakes, real-world consequences:

Why was I nervous? Well, because I knew we're not gonna be treated like high school no more. High school was like, if I wanted to do the work, I would do it; if I didn't want to, I won't do it. That's the deal. I'm still gonna pass anyway. High school was like, I'm gonna pass 'cause I'm gonna pass and college is like, you gotta earn your grade. I ain't gonna pass you, you're not gonna just sweet talk to the teacher and get that grade. So, and in high school, all it was was cheating. You'd be like, eh, I'm not gonna do anything, and then by the end of the class, it's like, "Hey, man, pass me the answers!" . . . and in college, it's like, pass me the answers and the professor's gonna be like, step out of the class, or something. So, my first day was like super nervous and my professors that I had was like, they were hard core, like mean. They were like you guys are not in high school no more, so don't even think about high school. We're in the real world. And open your books 'cause we're gonna . . . we're gonna start already, the lesson. And in high school, it was like three weeks after we start our first lesson and in college it's like your first day you're gonna start.

Several students also said they perceived high school and college very differently. As the preceding comment indicates, high school is seen as easier, and some men felt they could use their male privilege to charm their teachers or cheat to pass. Unfortunately, teachers and other students can also reinforce this culture of little or misdirected effort. A culture of protection (Kimmel, 2008) can shield young men from the realities of what it takes to succeed in education and can set them up for failure because they have not acquired the skills they need to succeed or the coping skills to deal with failure. Consequently, men often do not feel prepared for college-level work, which they take very seriously. They are also less likely to ask for help because they do not want to appear weak or compromise their appearance of confidence, as illustrated in the following from a male administrator:

> A lot of the students, you know, they won't ask for help. Since I've offered to help them and I've helped them, because sometimes they don't ask for it. Now, they know that, hey, there is somewhere I can go to, to get help or whatever it is that they need. All the students, I think that they need, they lack that, they won't go ask for help. We have to go and approach them and make the connection.

As this administrator makes clear, the issue is not necessarily that resources are unavailable or that students are uninformed of the resources or how to access them; the primary factor holding them back from seeking help is fear of appearing lazy or confused, or the desire to maintain pride in fulfilling their and their family's expectations without help. The concern at hand, therefore, is not one of just pride, but a mixture of pride and fear, which have proven a dangerous combination preventing many young Latino men from excelling academically. When men internalize traditional masculinity concepts, it can cause them to keep fear bottled up, and it can inhibit help-seeking behaviors.

An Example in Action

The preceding findings regarding the complex influence of pride and fear on educational experiences are only two examples of how traditional masculinity constructs are influencing the educational pathways of Latino males. As our research has developed, however, we have come to realize the limitations of using MGRC in our work. While MGRC is effective at labeling normative masculinity ideals, it does not move toward deconstructing masculinity. In addition, MGRC not only identifies masculinity constructs, it also implies there are normal and not normal masculine designations, such as the now-normalized notions of respect and reputation discussed by Gordon and Henery in Chapter 1. Since MGRC runs the risk of reifying normative characteristics, Chicana feminism is particularly useful for its willingness to strategically abandon normative categories and explore more fluid performances, bodies, spaces, and borderland crossings or intersectionalities (Calderón et al., 2012). To illustrate we provide an excerpt from our data followed by our initial analysis using MGRC with machismo and caballerismo, and then we reanalyze the same passage using a Chicana feminist perspective to illustrate how feminist methods can be employed productively in the study of men.

Excerpt from Data Using MGRC with Machismo and Caballerismo

Facilitator:	Do you think Latinos in general feel comfortable asking other Latinos for help, or is that . . .
Student #1:	I don't think so. I think there's some sort of pride in our culture that keeps us from asking for help in general.
Student #2:	Yeah, I think it's basically that some of us are on our own and we're by ourselves already so there's not really—we're already here doing this by ourselves, why do we need somebody to . . .
Student #3:	I heard a word that relates to that and they call it *machismo*.
Student #4:	Yeah, exactly.
Group:	[Laughs]
Student #3:	Yeah, trying to go out there and do it by yourself and not asking for help; that's one of the terms that I hear.
Student #1:	That's true.
Student #5:	And like what you were saying the *machismo*, when I would hear stories about my dad, he would tell me about how he raised us and that he didn't need help from anybody. So when I'm in school I'm thinking I have to do everything by myself because I have something to prove, and asking for help I guess kind of weakens the cause of what I'm doing. So there is some sense of *machismo* in that.

This passage is quite rich, and MGRC combined with machismo and caballerismo allowed us to identify the culturally specific masculinity scripts these young men were using. We noted that "the conversation begins and ends in restriction," and that men's pride—whether it was of self, culture, or family—prevented them from asking for help (Sáenz et al., 2012, p. 15). In addition, men commented "doing this [education]" alone was a key motivation for continuing alone; in other words, they want to retain control and maintain pride in individualistic action, which feeds into notions of competition. We also noted that Student #5 paid particular attention to his family context and wanted to live commensurate with his father's trajectory, "on his own and without help," showing the level of socialization he has experienced supporting his idea that alone is best (p. 15). We were also able to highlight how machismo interacted with the masculinity ideas of power and control, and we noted, "These young men see themselves as in control via their machismo" (p. 15).

The reader will note that in the preceding analysis we are able to pinpoint (or diagnose) the effect of patriarchal, hegemonic socialization, and in the case of Student #5, we were able to identify a partial source of his socialization as well: his father. In truth, though, where does this analysis take us? If this were Bloom's taxonomy, we would be in the lowest level of analysis: identification. In essence, we say: "Here's one! Here's another one!" but are unable to push beyond a superficial understanding of what's really going on in the conversation.

Excerpt from Data Using a Chicana Feminist Lens

In reanalyzing the passage through a Chicana feminist lens (Anzaldúa, 1987; Calderón et al., 2012), we found three powerful and immediate connections to Chicana feminism that helped us (re)think through patriarchy's influence on these young men. We first recognized the binary these young men were describing: Educational behaviors were seen as machismo or not machismo, a colonizing thought pattern of patriarchy. Second, we found that although the space created by the interview suggested a potential for *nepantla* (border crossing) and *coyolxauhqui* (a healing of bodymindspirit) (Anzaldúa, 1987), this space was not realized. Third, we were able to recognize the power of the colonial mythology of patriarchy in preventing a healing of bodymindspirit.

The young men in the study (Sáenz et al., 2012) have created a categorical binary: machismo and not machismo. They define *machismo* through heteronormative characteristics, as identified in the previous analysis, while *not machismo* is defined by what is considered feminine (although they never speak of feminization of educational spaces, their binary thinking leaves this as the unsaid, and therefore a meaningful and othered category). And so, this binary also represents a schism in the bodymindspirit (Anzaldúa, 1987). The mind seems focused on success and achievement, while the body and possibly the spirit are torn apart by categories that demand particular normative performances, normative silences, and compulsory heteronormative laughter at each other's pain. In this way, these young men dishonor their own internal voices, minimizing ostensible hurt through laughter but injuring the spirit by disrupting their own ways of knowing.

In addition, the space created by the focus group itself has also become a border-crossing space, a nepantla (Anzaldúa, 1987). The young men cross boundaries of masculinity and culture by inhabiting educational and research spaces and by contributing their unique voices and experiences. However, the presence of nepantla does not necessitate that the border-crossing space is fully used. Indeed, the separation between researcher and researched, as shown in the excerpt where the researcher asks a question and awaits response, as well as in the young men's laughter, suggests that while this space has created opportunity for border crossing, it did not coalesce and lead the young men to finding a fully voiced consciousness; in other words, this dialogue reveals patriarchy is still a colonizing presence through its demand of heteronormative performances in this gendered, all-male space.

Student #5's concluding thoughts also give us insight into the absence of *coyolxauhqui*. He elaborates about the role of his father's story in his own life, suggesting that his father's narrative of "standing alone" is not just narrative but also mythology. This narrative, a more specific story attached to the mythology of patriarchy as a force of power, control, and strength, has foreclosed the possibility of the emergence of a healing narrative. Rather than seeking an articulation of their own unique voices and stories, these young men rely on a mythology of the power of machismo to propel them forward (or should we say backward?).

Chicana feminism would also aid in addressing the question of how these young men's bodies are read in educational spaces and even in the research space created in the focus group; however, our data are not equipped to answer or examine this question. The laughter indicates a level of policing that makes the young men uncomfortable. Whether that policing is emanating from the presence of other men in general, the researcher or researchers, or a combination of the two, however, is unclear.

These young men, then, have been colonized by normative notions of masculinity. Their scripts are predetermined, and, although they are uncomfortable and working to silence their voices, they are also fighting for economic independence through education. Unfortunately, the very discomfort that speaking of machismo induces indicates that while this is an incipient space to allow for bodymindspirit healing, the space in which these young men exist daily is a place in the margins, called *el mundo zurdo* (Anzaldúa, 1987). This is in part by choice, but one that seems to have been made for them by the colonization of normative masculinity in their daily lives. Our recognition of the unrealized potential of this space as well as the simultaneous retelling of a colonizing mythology of patriarchy helped us realize the need to create spaces more expressly and openly address the dynamics of power, gender, race, and class throughout education. Researchers, professionals, and policymakers must aid in disrupting colonized and colonizing discourses to help male students and their allies become more socially aware and active in the deconstruction of colonizing patriarchy and its negative effects on men (Calderón et al., 2012).

This empirical and theoretical work has also found a practical outlet. In the next section we turn to a description of Project MALES (Mentoring to Achieve Latino Educational Success), a male-centered initiative that seeks news ways of addressing male achievement by applying the findings of our research.

Project MALES: A New Model of Male-Centered Initiative

Started in 2010, the Project MALES (http://ddce.utexas.edu/projectmales/) program at the University of Texas at Austin fosters discussion and relationship building among male and female undergraduate mentors and males of color in local high schools. The model is a research-informed initiative that highlights mentoring as a way to leverage social capital among males of color at various points in the educational pipeline to ultimately build a stronger college-going culture among this group of students. The basic structure entails a near-peer-mentoring philosophy, with college students being paired with high school students to allow long-term bonds to develop.

The mentoring model takes a dynamic and intergenerational approach to achieve increased achievement and retention of male students of color in secondary and postsecondary educational settings. This model brings together three key groups: professionals and graduate students as role models, Latino or African American college students (upperclassmen and first year), and younger Latino and African American male students in local high schools. In this model, professionals (e.g., graduate students, student affairs professionals, community leaders, and allies) serve as mentors to males of color in college. In turn, these college students have the opportunity to engage in mentoring local high school male students. This intergenerational model is structured around a variety of experiences that focus on leadership development, community engagement, and service. The following are formal activities of our mentoring program:

- Weekly or biweekly guided, purposeful peer-mentoring sessions across generational lines (professionals to college students, college students to high school students). The 1-hour weekly or biweekly sessions between college students and high school students focus on topics such as the college application process, college choice options, financial aid options, study skills and time management, the life of a college student, and choosing a college major.

- Weekly meetings among first-year college students (a cohort-style experience) to strengthen social bonds and cultivate a nurturing network between mentor participants. These sessions are used to discuss and train students on mentoring topics for each week, discuss issues of masculinity and identity, discuss issues of gender equity, and generally cultivate a safe and nurturing space for our students.

- A monthly Pláticas, or fireside chat, series featuring prominent male speakers (e.g., professionals, graduate students, role models) who facilitate small-group discussions among mentor participants. This monthly chat facilitates mentoring links between professional mentors (e.g., grad students, faculty, and community leaders) and our Project MALES students. The strategy is to pair our student mentors with professional mentors to fully leverage the intergenerational nature of our mentoring structure.

- Semester-long community outreach and service projects involving mentors and protégés at participating colleges and school districts. Many of these activities already include participating in various community-wide education forums and other service opportunities.

Practical Implications of Our Work on Latino Males

This section highlights key implications for practice that we have distilled from our research findings (Sáenz et al., 2012). These implications are written with an eye toward existing efforts, and our aim is to continue to inform the strong commitment that has already been demonstrated to the issue of Latino male student success.

First-Year Programs with Men in Mind

The ability of a first-year Latino male college student to successfully navigate the complex college environment can be critical to his success through graduation. First-year programs with men in mind represent an immediate positive mechanism to assist Latino males in being successful not only in college but also after college. Programming with men in mind can provide meaningful opportunities for Latino males to socialize with other Latino males in college and to develop purposeful relationships with male faculty and staff. These programs are important because male students often do not seek assistance, tend to believe they can figure things out on their own, and can even be inadvertently stigmatized by special programs. Latino-male-based programs during the first year can provide institutions with appropriate safe spaces for Latino males to learn what is important about being successful in college as well as provide the necessary support services with their specific needs in mind. Programs such as these should seek to create opportunities for border crossing and healing bodymindspirit experiences for young men, emphasizing fluidity and acceptance of difference rather than reifying the colonizing, and policing, of men's behaviors and bodies (Calderón et al., 2012).

High-Stakes Engagement

High-stakes engagement refers to the critical period when a student first interacts with the institution, and the institution responds to that interaction. The outcome of that encounter can determine whether the institution has lost its first and only chance to make a true connection. Latino male students, like most college students who believe an institution is not engaging them or providing useful support services, are likely not to return for additional support services or to the institution. Therefore, institutional staff, faculty, and administrators must be prepared to engage and be responsive to Latino male students. When Latino males reach out for help, support needs to be immediately provided, or the opportunity to connect might possibly be lost. Furthermore, staff, faculty, and administrators must make themselves available to young Latino men *early* and *often*. Since men are less likely to ask for help, when advisers are faced with silence they should assume a student is lacking in knowledge. At worst, students will receive redundant information, and, at best, students will become more involved with their course work and gain vital information they need to succeed. High-stakes engagement specifically refers to the environment many Latino males inhabit in educational spaces—el mundo zurdo, or the place in the margins where the dispossessed and subaltern exist (Anzaldúa, 1987). These first interactions can help bridge this space by creating a sense of community and a support structure that welcome young men instead of colonizing them further.

Role Models Matter

Time and time again, Latino male students indicated they do not see enough Latino male role models on campus. Role modeling matters because students get the opportunity to see someone like them who is successful. Role models can play a pivotal role in the success of Latino male students because they increase student social networking knowledge and skills; connect students to mentors (male alumni, faculty, or staff); offer real-world experiences through a caring, trusting, and safe environment; and provide pathways for positive reinforcement for successful decisions as well as constructive feedback for correcting poor decisions. Role modeling also allows successful Latino male adults to connect with college Latino male students and give back to their communities in meaningful ways. Adults, male and female, need to connect with younger men who are looking for guidance and direction. Although anyone can be a role model, for Latino male students it is important that successful males talk to male students. Latino male students should be provided with the opportunity to understand how to be successful and to see themselves being successful. Role models play a particularly important role in creating opportunities for a healing of bodymindspirit (Anzaldúa, 1987) by providing safe spaces, honoring students' voices, and critically pushing against mythologies of patriarchy and colonialization.

Messaging to Latino Males and Their Families

The message Latino males and their families receive about attending college and completing a college degree needs to be more realistic (i.e., college is not easy, it requires time and energy, and it is challenging). We need to flip the switch about what it really means to go to college and be honest about the sacrifices necessary to be successful in college. The drive to get more students to attend college typically comes with the message that anyone can go to college, or anyone has the potential to earn a college degree; however, unless that message comes with a clear understanding of what it really takes to complete college and get a degree, the message may be lost on male students and their families and can lead to disenchantment with college and to the student dropping out.

Furthermore, many male students are competitive. Educators need to tap into the male competitive spirit without encouraging competition among men or between Latinos and Latinas. Latino male students need to be told that there are no shortcuts to earning a college degree and that what they are doing is difficult. Latino male students need to understand most of them will have to work while earning a college degree, and that is just their reality. This form of messaging helps male students split time judiciously between work and college and lets them know it is okay to work and contribute to the family's income and still go to college. It is possible, and it is worth it. By leveraging a student's competitive spirit in the pursuit of a college degree, one can ignite his internal drive for success. Of course, tapping into a competitive drive also requires an explicit discussion of how to cope with failure. Since Latino males are disinclined to ask for help or to admit imminent failure, previously mentioned strategies such as creating safe spaces for discussion and strategic advising must equip men with the skills and the mind-set to respond to failure constructively.

In branding the message of college completion to Latino males, institutions need to inform them of the reality of their existence as a population in college. Latino males need to know that their population tends not to be successful in college, but that their success in college is the mechanism for changing that reality as well as paving the path for future Latino males. Latino males need to be informed how their success can be an inspiration for other Latino males to be successful. This kind of messaging can help them understand that they may be arriving at the doors of education from the position of el mundo zurdo but also that they have a role to play in the broader social development of their people and their families.

Family Influence: Fathers, Mothers, Siblings, Others

Educational institutions (P–16) need to develop policies that encourage families to become actively involved in their Latino males' educational experience. School administrators need to be especially sensitive to the economic drivers that constantly tantalize young Latino males to join the workforce, especially if they come from low-income or working-class backgrounds. One strategy is to acknowledge this reality and impress upon students the importance of persisting and finishing college. Another key strategy is to educate families—especially parental figures—about the potential for increased economic returns that can come from a son's sacrifice of delaying entry into the full-time workforce until after the degree is earned. Educating institutional agents and families about Latino males' challenges can also serve to create more supportive environments that allow more fluidity of performance and exact less of a colonial toll on men's behaviors.

Concluding Thoughts on Reframing the Study of Men

Through decades of political, social, and theoretical work, feminists and their allies have transformed the landscape of gender equity in America. Though we still have a long way to go to achieve gender equity in many areas, one cannot deny that progress has been made. Despite studies on men dating from as far back as the 1970s, studies on men as men have not flourished in part because the concept of masculinity is still often naturalized and normalized through social systems and pop culture.

It would be erroneous, however, to pit gender equity agendas against each other. This is not an oppression olympics (as Gordon and Henery discuss in Chapter 1), and although there has been a recent tendency to position men as the victims of women's success (see Yakaboski, 2011), there should be no losers in gender equity. This requires a careful reframing of the gender equity debate. Indeed, multiple domains of men's and women's lives have the potential of finding interest convergence as well as ways to speak across the table on contentious issues (e.g., parental rights) and speak in chorus on issues of convergence (e.g., health, domestic violence, sexual harassment).

The 21st century is a complex world for young men and women to navigate, and using feminist methods in the study of men would aid in disrupting the naturalization of White middle-class heteronormative masculinity, deconstructing what constitutes masculinity for various groups, subgroups, and individuals, and problemize the social institutions that serve to perpetuate negative normative constructions of masculinity. We have had a name for patriarchal masculinity for quite some time, but until we recognize its harmful effects on men and women alike, little is likely to change.

Finally, it is essential to recognize and acknowledge that we can no longer remain silent about this growing educational crisis facing Latino males and other males of color. We believe that for Latino males to succeed in the varied educational pathways, researchers, policymakers, public officials, private sector leaders, and Latino families and communities have to embrace this social justice and gender equity agenda. The sobering statistics are a clarion call for proactive action. We are compelled to raise awareness of this issue at all levels of education—P–12, postsecondary, and workforce development—but we are also compelled to act. There is a pressing need to address this issue because Latino males represent an untapped resource in our intellectual marketplace. We need to illuminate the importance of educational policies and practices that assist and support Latino males in the educational system.

Note

1. We must note that within the feminist movement, some factions support the men's movement and some factions call for radical changes in power structures to empower women while disempowering men. The same opinion splits exist within the men's movement in reverse, with a small group seeking to return women to the Victorian period and the cult of domesticity; however, these radical subgroups are not the majority in either gender movement.

References

Anzaldúa, G. (1987). *Borderlands, la frontera: The new mestizo.* San Francisco, CA: Aunt Lute Books.

Arciniega, G. M., Anderson, T. C., Tovar-Blank, Z. G., & Tracey, T. J. G. (2008). Toward a fuller conception of machismo: Development of a traditional machismo and caballerismo scale. *Journal of Counseling Psychology, 55*(1), 19–33.

Bartlett, K. T., & Rhode, D. L. (2009). *Gender and law: Theory, doctrine, commentary* (5th ed.). New York, NY: Aspen.

Battiste, M. (2008). Research ethics for protecting indigenous knowledge and heritage: Institutional and researcher responsibilities. In N. K. Denzin, Y. S. Lincoln, & L. T. Smith (Eds.), *Handbook of critical and indigenous methodologies* (pp. 497–510). Thousand Oaks, CA: Sage.

Brah, A., & Phoenix, A. (2004). Ain't I a woman? Revisiting intersectionality. *Journal of International Women's Studies*, 5(3), 75–86.

Brannon, R. (1976). The male sex role: Our culture's blueprint for manhood, what it's done for us lately. In D. David & R. Brannon (Eds.), *The forty-nine percent majority: The male sex role* (pp. 1–49). Reading, MA: Addison-Wesley.

Butler, J. (1993). *Bodies that matter: On the discursive limits of "sex."* New York, NY: Routledge.

Butler, J. (2004). *Undoing gender*. New York, NY: Routledge.

Calderón, D., Delgado Bernal, D., Pérez Huber, L., Malagón, M. C., & Nelly Vélez, V. (2012). A Chicana feminist epistemology revisited: Cultivating ideas a generation later. *Harvard Educational Review*, 82(4), 513–539.

Campbell, A. L. (2004). *Raising the bar: Ruth Bader Ginsburg and the ACLU Women's Rights Project*. Bloomington, IN: Xlibris.

Cole, E. R. (2009). Intersectionality and research in psychology. *American Psychologist*, 64(3), 170–180. doi:10.1037/a0014564

College Board. (2011). The educational experience of young men of color: Capturing the student voice. Retrieved from http://youngmenofcolor.collegeboard.org/sites/default/files/downloads/EEYMC-StudentVoice.pdf

Collins, P. H. (2000). *Black feminist thought: Knowledge, consciousness, and the politics of empowerment* (2nd ed.). New York, NY: Routledge.

Combahee River Collective. (1981). A Black feminist statement. In C. Moraga, G. Anzaldúa, & T. C. Bambara (Eds.), *This bridge called my back: Writing by radical women of color* (pp. 210–218). Watertown, MA: Persephone Press.

Connell, R. W. (1995). *Masculinities*. Cambridge, UK: Polity Press.

Cree, V. E., & Cavanagh, K. (1996). Men, masculinism and social work. In K. Cavanagh & V. E. Cree (Eds.), *Working with men: Feminism and social work* (pp. 1–8). New York, NY: Routledge.

Crenshaw, K. (1991). Mapping the margins: Intersectionality, identity politics, and violence against women of color. *Stanford Law Review*, 43(6), 1241–1299.

Crouch, H. (2011). *History of the Coalition of Free Men, Inc.* (NCFM). Retrieved July 13, 2012, from http://ncfm.org/lead-with-us/history/

Davis, T. L. (2010). Voices of gender role conflict: The social construction of college men's identity. In S. R. Harper & F. Harris, III (Eds.), *College men and masculinities: Theory, research, and implications for practice* (pp. 49–65). San Francisco, CA: Jossey-Bass.

de Beauvoir, S. (2011). *The second sex* (C. Borde & S. Malovany-Chevallier, Trans). New York, NY: Vintage Books. (Original work published 1949)

De La Cancela, V. (1981). *Towards a critical psychological analysis of machismo: Puerto Ricans and mental health* (Doctoral dissertation). Available from ProQuest Dissertations and Theses database. (No. 303113722)

De La Cancela, V. (1993). "Coolin": The psychosocial communication of African and Latino men. *Urban League Review, 16*(2), 33–44.

Denzin, N. K. (2003). *Performance ethnography: Critical pedagogy and the politics of culture.* Thousand Oaks, CA: Sage.

Dill, B. T., & Zambrana, R. E. (2009). Critical thinking about inequality: An emerging lens. In B. T. Dill & R. E. Zambrana (Eds.), *Emerging intersections: Race, class, and gender in theory, policy, and practice* (pp. 1–21). New Brunswick, NJ: Rutgers University Press.

Dillard, C. B., & Okpalaoka, C. (2011). The sacred and spiritual nature of endarkened transnational feminist praxis in qualitative research. In N. K. Denzin & Y. S. Lincoln (Eds.), *The Sage handbook of qualitative research* (4th ed., pp. 147–162). Thousand Oaks, CA: Sage.

Elenes, C. A. (2011). *Transforming borders: Chicana/o popular culture and pedagogy.* Lanham, MD: Lexington Books.

Ennis, S. R., Rios-Vargas, M., & Albert, N. G. (2011). *The Hispanic population: 2010.* Washington, DC: U.S. Census Bureau, U.S. Department of Commerce, Economics and Statistics Administration.

Ferdman, B. M., & Gallegos, P. I. (2001). Racial identity development and Latinos in the United States. In C. L. Wijeyesinghe & B. W. Jackson, III (Eds.), *New perspectives on racial identity development: A theoretical and practical anthology* (pp. 32–66). New York, NY: NYU Press.

Freedman, E. B. (2002). *No turning back: The history of feminism and the future of women.* New York, NY: Ballantine.

Friedan, B. (1964). *The feminine mystique.* New York, NY: Norton.

Gloria, A. M., Castellanos, J., Scull, N. C., & Villegas, F. J. (2009). Psychological coping and well-being of male Latino undergraduates. *Hispanic Journal of Behavioral Sciences, 31*(3), 317–339. doi:10.1177/0739986309336845

Harding, S. (2008). *Sciences from below: Feminisms, postcolonialities, and modernities.* Durham, NC: Duke University Press.

Harper, S. R., Carini, R. M., Bridges, B. K., & Hayek, J. C. (2004). Gender differences in student engagement among African American undergraduates at historically Black colleges and universities. *Journal of College Student Development, 45*(3), 271–284.

Harper, S. R., & Harris, F., III (Eds.). (2010). *College men and masculinities: Theory, research, and implications for practice.* San Francisco, CA: Jossey-Bass.

Harris, F., III, & Harper, S. R. (2008). Masculinities go to community college: Understanding male identity socialization and gender role conflict. *New Directions for Community Colleges, 142,* 25–35.

Harris, F., III, & Martin, B. E. (2006). Examining productive conceptions of masculinities: Lessons learned from academically driven African American male student-athletes. *The Journal of Men's Studies, 14*(3), 359–378.

Hennessy, R., & Ingraham, C. (1997). Introduction: Reclaiming anticapitalist feminism. In R. Hennessy & C. Ingraham (Eds.), *Materialist feminism: A reader in class, difference, and women's lives* (pp. 1–16). New York, NY: Routledge.

hooks, b. (2000). *Feminist theory: From margin to center* (2nd ed.). Cambridge, MA: South End Press.

Josselson, R., & Harway, M. (2012). The challenges of multiple identity. In R. Josselson & M. Harway (Eds.), *Navigating multiple identities: Race, gender, culture, nationality, and roles* (pp. 3–12). New York, NY: Oxford University Press.

Kaufman, M. (1999). Men, feminism, and men's contradictory experiences of power. In J. A. Kuypers (Ed.), *Men and power* (pp. 59–85). Halifax, Nova Scotia: Fernwood Books.

Kimmel, M. (2008). *Guyland: The perilous world where boys become men.* New York, NY: HarperCollins.

Kimmel, M. S., & Davis, T. (2011). Mapping guyland in college. In J. A. Laker & T. Davis (Eds.), *Masculinities in higher education: Theoretical and practical considerations* (pp. 3–15). New York, NY: Routledge.

Lewis, R. A. (1981). Men's liberation and the men's movement: Implications for counselors. *Personnel and Guidance Journal, 60*(4), 256–259.

Mahalik, J. R., Englar-Carlson, M., & Good, G. E. (2003). Masculinity scripts, presenting concerns, and help seeking: Implications for practice and training. *Professional Psychology: Research and Practice, 34*(2), 123–131.

Meth, R. L., & Pasick, R. S. (1990). *Men in therapy: The challenge of change.* New York, NY: Guilford Press.

Mirandé, A. (1997). *Hombres y machos: Masculinity and Latino culture.* Boulder, CO: Westview Press.

Olesen, V. (2011). Feminist qualitative research in the millennium's first decade: Developments, challenges, prospects. In N. K. Denzin & Y. S. Lincoln (Eds.), *The Sage handbook of qualitative research* (4th ed., pp. 129–146). Thousand Oaks, CA: Sage.

O'Neil, J. M. (1981). Male sex role conflicts, sexism, and masculinity: Psychological implications for men, women, and the counseling psychologist. *Counseling Psychologist, 9*(2), 61–80.

Pollack, W. S. (1999). The sacrifice of Isaac: A new psychology of boys and men. *Society for the Psychological Study of Men and Masculinity Bulletin, 4,* 7–14.

Pollack, W. S., & Shuster, T. (2001). *Real boys' voices.* New York, NY: Penguin.

Ramírez, R. L. (1999). *What it means to be a man: Reflections on Puerto Rican masculinity* (R. E. Casper, Trans.). New Brunswick, NJ: Rutgers University Press.

Richmond, K. A., Levant, R. F., & Ladhani, S. C. J. (2012). The varieties of the masculine experience. In R. Josselson & M. Harway (Eds.), *Navigating multiple identities: Race, gender, culture, nationality, and roles* (pp. 59–74). New York, NY: Oxford University Press.

Rodriguez, R., & Gonzales, P. (1997). *Deconstructing machismo.* Retrieved July 13, 2012, from http://www.azteca.net/aztec/literat/macho.html

Rubin, G. S. (2011). *A Gayle Rubin reader.* Durham, NC: Duke University Press.

Sáenz, V. B., Bukoski, B., Lu, C., & Rodriguez, S. (2012, November). *Latino males in Texas community colleges: A phenomenological study of masculinity constructs and their effect on college experiences.* Paper presented at the meeting of the Association for the Study of Higher Education, Las Vegas, NV.

Sáenz, V. B., & Ponjuan, L. (2009). The vanishing Latino male in higher education. *Journal of Hispanic Higher Education, 8*(1), 54–89.

Sáenz, V. B., & Ponjuan, L. (2011). *Men of color: Ensuring the academic success of Latino males in higher education.* Retrieved July 10, 2012, from http://www.ihep .org/assets/files/publications/m-r/(Brief)_Men_of_Color_Latinos.pdf

Schneir, M. (1994). *Feminism: The essential historical writings.* New York, NY: Vintage Books.

Sommers, C. H. (2000). *The war against boys: How misguided feminism is harming our young men.* New York, NY: Simon & Schuster.

Sullivan, N. (2003). *A critical introduction to queer theory.* New York, NY: NYU Press.

Torres, J. B., Solberg, V. S. H., & Carlstrom, A. H. (2002). The myth of sameness among Latino men and their machismo. *American Journal of Orthopsychiatry, 72*(2), 163–181.

Tyre, P. (2006). *The trouble with boys.* Retrieved July 13, 2012, from http://www .thedailybeast.com/newsweek/2006/01/29/the-trouble-with-boys.html

U.S. Constitution, Amendment XIX.

Wagner, R. (2011). Embracing liberatory practice: Promoting men's development as a feminist act. In J. A. Laker & T. Davis (Eds.), *Masculinities in higher education: Theoretical and practical considerations* (pp. 210–223). New York, NY: Routledge.

Wilson, R. (2007). The new gender divide. *The Chronicle of Higher Education, 53*(21), A36.

Wood, J. T. (2011). *Gendered lives: Communication, gender and culture.* Boston, MA: Wadsworth.

Yakaboski, T. (2011). Quietly stripping the pastels: The undergraduate gender gap. *The Review of Higher Education, 34*(4), 555–580.

5

(RE)SETTING THE AGENDA FOR COLLEGE MEN OF COLOR

Lessons Learned from a 15-Year Movement to Improve Black Male Student Success

Shaun R. Harper

ordon, Gordon, and Nembhard (1994) and Brown (2011) highlight consistent themes in the social science literature on Black men in America. In these syntheses of studies published over several decades, these authors critique the hopelessness of this population as portrayed in media, books, academic research journals, and the collective imagination of U.S. citizens and others across the globe. They also problemize how Black men are routinely characterized as an endangered species and a group in crisis or at risk in various social milieu. Brown cites publications that date from the 1930s. Accordingly, pathological discourses that caricature Black men as lazy, incompetent, untrustworthy, and undeserving of respectability in our society are not new. Erik Eckholm's (2006) article in *The New York Times*, "Plight Deepens for Black Men, Studies Warn," reinforced much of what previous generations of scholars and journalists have repeatedly offered.

Consistent with writings in other disciplines, Harper and Davis (2012) conclude that years of published research on Black male students at all levels of education advance one long-standing narrative: They don't care about school. Specifically concerning higher education scholarship and practice,

Harper (2009) argues, "Anyone who takes time to read about them could confidently conclude that Black male undergraduates are troubled, their future is bleak, they all do poorly, and there is little that can be done to reverse long-standing outcomes disparities that render them among the least likely to succeed in college" (pp. 699–700).

Again, this depressing narrative is persistent and pervasive. It has been documented over and over again, and at this point it is unlikely to be surprising to most Americans within and outside the race.

Despite the durability of deficit-oriented narratives about Black male students in education and society, social panic concerning their educational attainment and outcomes in postsecondary institutional contexts seems to have worsened over a 15-year period (1997–2012). In particular, educators and administrators, as well as philanthropic organizations and professional associations, have become increasingly fascinated with the status of Black undergraduate men. Michael J. Cuyjet's (1997) "Helping African American Men Succeed in College" did much to raise consciousness among various stakeholders in higher education. Four years later, the magazine *Black Issues in Higher Education* (now *Diverse Issues in Higher Education*) posed an attention-grabbing question on its front cover, "How Much Does Higher Education Matter to Black Males?" that corresponds with an article inside by Roach (2001). That question and others like it have since been at the center of local and national conversations among postsecondary actors; much has been done on college campuses and elsewhere to improve Black undergraduate men's success. Notwithstanding, their enrollments, academic performance, and rates of baccalaureate degree attainment remain just as troublesome now as they were 15 years ago. But why? And what can be learned as various stakeholders introduce future initiatives in response to issues affecting Black undergraduate men, as well as Asian American/Pacific Islander (AAPI), Latino, and Native American male collegians?

This chapter chronicles the 15-year emphasis on Black male students in U.S. higher education. It first catalogs a range of efforts enacted between 1997 and 2012, and then explores why Black male student enrollments, engagement, and degree attainment rates remained relatively unchanged. This examination of the shortcomings and shortsightedness of these efforts could prove instructive for educators and administrators who attempt to improve outcomes among college men of color. Noteworthy is that Latino, AAPI, and Native American undergraduate men combined have received less attention than Black male collegians over the past decade and a half. Hence, this chapter is based on a movement intended to improve Black male student success but concludes with recommendations for future efforts aimed at all four groups, individually and collectively.

Cataloging a 15-Year Frenzy

Jackson and Moore (2008) raised questions about the burgeoning response to a so-called crisis among Black male students in education. Specifically, they asked if recent efforts were by-products of "popular media infatuation" (p. 847), or if educators, policymakers, and concerned others were authentically committed to enacting the structural changes required to reverse long-standing trends. In 2008 Open Society Foundations (OSF) introduced its Campaign for Black Male Achievement, which aims to address the social, political, economic, and educational forces that negatively affect outcomes for Black American boys and men. Three years later, OSF pledged $30 million to the New York City Young Men's Initiative, while the city of New York committed $67.5 million and Bloomberg Philanthropies, $30 million (Harper & Associates, in press). According to Shah and Sato (2012), total annual foundation donations for Black men and boys increased from $10.8 million in 2003 to $28.6 million in 2010, but education investments have been disproportionately concentrated at the elementary, middle, and high school levels. Statistics presented in reports on the condition of Black male students in the early stages of the educational pipeline (e.g., Lewis, Simon, Uzzell, Horwitz, & Casserly, 2010; Schott Foundation for Public Education, 2010; Toldson, 2008, 2011; Toldson & Lewis, 2012) justify the rise in philanthropic spending on K–12 school endeavors. Comparatively, efforts focusing squarely on Black male student success in postsecondary educational contexts have been haphazard and not as well funded.

From 1997 onward, Black male undergraduates have increasingly become a fascinating unit of analysis among researchers and a topic of discussion among professionals at conferences and elsewhere in higher education. For example, more than 70 sessions about the Black undergraduate were presented at annual conferences of the American College Personnel Association and the National Association of Student Personnel Administrators during the 15-year period; additional presentations were made at other national meetings for postsecondary educators and administrators. It seems that from one year to the next, more and more highly educated and seemingly well-intentioned people were convinced that something needed to be done about the alarming underrepresentation of Black men among collegegoers and degree earners.

Writings about the challenges confronting Black undergraduate men have been plentiful. Scholars, whose aims were to raise consciousness about these students and subsequently ignite a range of institutional responses, have surely succeeded. More has been written about Black male collegians over the past 15 years than any other specific racialized sex group in higher education (including Black women, White undergraduate men, and other groups of minoritized male students). Table 5.1 lists 11 books published since 1997.

TABLE 5.1
Books on Black Undergraduate Men Published Between
1997 and 2012

Authors/Editors	No. of Pages
Bonner (2010)	217
Byrne (2006)	236
Cuyjet (1997)	110
Cuyjet (2006)	384
Dancy (2012)	220
Frierson, Pearson, & Wyche (2009)	336
Frierson, Wyche, & Pearson (2009)	365
Hilton, Wood, & Lewis (2012)	242
Jones (2004)	178
Palmer & Wood (2012)	224
Ross (1998)	160

Bonner (2010), Dancy (2012), Jones (2004), and Ross (1998) are single-authored texts; the others are edited volumes that brought together several scholars from multiple institutions to contribute chapters on various aspects of Black men's experiences and outcomes across a range of institution types. Byrne's (2006) book focuses specifically on historically Black colleges and universities (HBCUs), whereas each chapter in Hilton et al.'s (2012) book is devoted to Black men in a particular postsecondary context (e.g., community colleges, religiously affiliated institutions, and for-profit universities). Cuyjet's (2006) book also includes nine chapters that showcase various institutional initiatives aimed at Black undergraduate men.

In addition to the 2,672 pages of these 11 books, researchers published more than 60 articles in peer-reviewed academic journals between 1997 and 2012. Some of these empirical studies focused more broadly on Black undergraduate men overall (e.g., Dancy, 2011; Dancy & Brown, 2008; Harper & Nichols, 2008; Harris, Palmer, & Struve, 2011; Jackson, 2012; Smith, Allen, & Danley, 2007; Strayhorn, 2008a, 2008b), while others concentrated on specific subgroups and unique institutional environments (namely, HBCUs and community colleges). Twenty-five examples of the latter, including some details about the research methods on which each article is based, are presented in Table 5.2. As shown, the overwhelming majority were single-institution qualitative studies with an average of 27 participants (who in almost every

TABLE 5.2

Select Peer-Reviewed Journal Articles on Black Undergraduate Men

Subgroup/Sector	Article	Site(s)	Research Method	Sample Size
Achievers and student leaders	Bonner (2003)	Multiple (2)	Qualitative	2
	Harper (2009)	Multiple (30)	Qualitative	143
	Harper & Quaye (2007)	Multiple (6)	Qualitative	32
	Harper et al. (2011)	Multiple (6)	Qualitative	52
	Martin & Harris (2006)	Multiple (4)	Qualitative	27
Community colleges	Glenn (2004)	Multiple (2)	Mixed	n/a
	Hagedorn, Maxwell, & Hampton (2002)	Single	Quantitative	202
	Wood (2012)	Multiple	Quantitative	2,235
	Wood, Hilton, & Lewis (2011)	Multiple	Quantitative	575
	Wood & Turner (2011)	Single	Qualitative	28
Gay/bisexual men	Goode-Cross & Good (2009)	Single	Qualitative	7
	Goode-Cross & Tager (2011)	Single	Qualitative	8
	Patton (2011)	Single	Qualitative	6
	Strayhorn, Blakewood, & DeVita (2008)	Single	Qualitative	7
	Strayhorn & Mullins (2012)	Multiple (6)	Qualitative	29

Subgroup/Sector	Article	Site(s)	Research Method	Sample Size
HBCUs	Harper & Gasman (2008)	Multiple (12)	Qualitative	76
	Palmer, Davis, and Hilton (2009)	Single	Qualitative	11
	Riggins, McNeal, & Herndon (2008)	Single	Qualitative	13
	Rodney, Tachia, & Rodney (1997)	Multiple (11)	Quantitative	1,874
	Washington, Wang, & Browne (2009)	Multiple (35)	Quantitative	1,865
Student athletes	Beamon & Bell (2006)	Single	Quantitative	100
	Benson (2000)	Single	Qualitative	8
	Oseguera (2010)	Single	Qualitative	17
	Sellers & Kuperminc (1997)	Multiple (42)	Quantitative	702
	Singer (2005)	Single	Qualitative	4

instance were interviewed only once). Empirical evidence concerning the status of Black undergraduate men was also furnished in a series of research reports (e.g., Harper, 2006; Harper, 2012; Harper & Harris, 2012; Harper, Williams, & Blackman, 2013). Additional writings pertaining to Black male collegians were published in edited books (e.g., Brown, Dancy, & Davis, 2013; Dancy & Brown, 2012; Polite & Davis, 1999; Zamani-Gallaher & Polite, 2010) and special theme issues of peer-reviewed academic journals (e.g., *The Journal of Men's Studies*, 2003; *Teachers College Record*, 2006; *American Behavioral Scientist*, 2008; *The Journal of Negro Education*, 2009; *Race Ethnicity and Education*, 2011) focusing on Black male students across all levels of education, from preschool through graduate school.

College and university administrators seem to have been persuaded, at least in part, by the preponderance of research published and presented at conferences between 1997 and 2012. It is also likely that alarming academic performance data, low persistence and graduation rates, and firsthand observations of Black male disengagement on their campuses compelled postsecondary professionals to act in myriad ways. Most common was the creation and implementation of mentoring programs that matched Black male college students with faculty, administrators, and staff on their campuses. Another common institutional activity was a 1- to 2-day summit that brought together stakeholders from across the campus and sometimes from multiple institutions in a city or region. The convening typically included remarks from the college president or chief diversity officer about the importance of the event, an inspiring keynote speaker, a series of workshops and panels (which rarely had student presenters), and meals. The cost of an event of this magnitude can easily exceed $20,000. Shown in Table 5.3 are some institutions that hosted Black male summits. University of Akron has hosted its summit annually since 2008, with nearly 1,000 attendees in 2012. The Minnesota Private College Council and the United Negro College Fund have hosted similar 1- to 2-day gatherings focused on Black undergraduate men.

Several colleges and universities across the United States created multidimensional Black male institutes, centers, and initiatives (see Table 5.4). These resources vary in design and scope; most offer, but extend far beyond, protégé-mentor matching and annual daylong summits. The Center for Male Engagement at the Community College of Philadelphia, for example, provides an actual space for students that includes computers and support coaches (full-time professionals who provide academic, personal, and career counseling). The Todd A. Bell National Resource Center at The Ohio State University hosts an annual retreat, a lecture series, and a luncheon that raises funds for student scholarships, an early arrival weekend for incoming Black male freshmen, and an annual ceremony to celebrate students who

TABLE 5.3
Select Campuses Hosting 1- to 2-Day Black Male Summits

Type	Institution
Community college	Coastline Community College
	Howard Community College
	Lone Star College–North Harris
	Merritt College
	Miami Dade College
Private 4 year	Denison University
	Gallaudet University
	Morehouse College
	Princeton University
	University of Denver
	Wake Forest University
Public 4 year	Eastern Illinois University
	Indiana University-Purdue University Indianapolis
	Louisiana State University
	Old Dominion University
	University of Akron
	University of Alabama at Birmingham
	University of California, Irvine
	University of Illinois at Chicago
	University of New Mexico
	University of Northern Iowa
	University of Texas at Austin
	University of West Florida
	Virginia Polytechnic Institute and State University
	Winston-Salem State University

TABLE 5.4
Select Black Male Centers, Institutes, and Initiatives

Initiative	*State*
Anne Arundel Community College Black Male Initiative	Maryland
Arkansas African American Male Initiative[a]	Arkansas
Cincinnati State Technical & Community College Black Male Initiative	Ohio
City University of New York Black Male Initiative[b]	New York
Community College of Philadelphia Center for Male Engagement	Pennsylvania
Midlands Technical College African American Male Leadership Institute	South Carolina
Morehouse College, The Morehouse Male Initiative	Georgia
North Carolina Central University African American Male Initiative	North Carolina
Philander Smith College Black Male Initiative	Arkansas
Prairie State College African American Male Initiative	Illinois
Sinclair Community College African-American Male Initiative	Ohio
St. Louis Community College African-American Male Initiative	Missouri
St. Philip's College African American Male Initiative	Texas
The Ohio State University Todd A. Bell National Resource Center	Ohio
University of California, Los Angeles Black Male Institute	California
University of Louisville African American Male Initiative	Kentucky
University of Maryland Black Male Initiative	Maryland
University System of Georgia African-American Male Initiative[b]	Georgia
University of Virginia Luther Porter Jackson Black Male Initiative	Virginia
University of Wisconsin Beyond the Game Initiative	Wisconsin

[a]Statewide initiative funded by the Winthrop Rockefeller Foundation unites seven community/technical colleges and 10 four-year institutions (including two HBCUs).
[b]Systemwide, multicampus initiatives.

achieve academic excellence. A structured course that acclimates first-year students to resources and introduces them to important people who can aid in their success is just one of many activities offered through the University of California, Los Angeles Black Male Institute. System-level efforts have emerged (e.g., the City University of New York's Black Male Initiative and the University System of Georgia's African American Male Initiative), and so too have statewide consortia such as the Arkansas African American Male Initiative. Finally, an incalculable number of clubs and organizations for Black undergraduate men (including over 200 chapters of the Student African American Brotherhood) were started on campuses across the United States between 1997 and 2012.

Publications and institutional activities listed in the four tables in this section represent only a fraction of everything done over a 15-year period to call attention to the needs of and issues faced by Black male students. The full catalog is much more extensive. Despite these efforts, Black male enrollment numbers remain sluggish in comparison to other groups, sex gaps in postsecondary degree attainment across all levels is most pronounced among Black students, and only one-third of Black men who start undergraduate degree programs at public 4-year institutions graduate within 6 years (Harper, 2012; Harper & Harris, 2012). Given the amount of attention devoted to this population, the stability of these trends seems counterintuitive. This raises two critical questions: Why has a decade and a half of multidimensional activity not yielded better results, and what should well-intentioned educators and policymakers keep in mind as they undertake new efforts to improve educational outcomes for all college men of color?

Some Weaknesses of the Movement

Scholars who study public policy often concern themselves with explaining gaps between the *intended* and *actual* effects of legislative actions, including the investment of public resources. Theirs is a useful approach for making sense of what happened in higher education between 1997 and 2012 on behalf of Black undergraduate men. Individually and collectively, the intent of activities described in the previous section was to raise consciousness and subsequently improve the status of a population. Consequently, U.S. higher education should have experienced gradual upticks in Black male student enrollment and rates of postsecondary educational attainment. For myriad reasons, this has not occurred. Explanations are manifold; a half dozen are offered next.

Flimsy Strategy, Missing Standards

Many well-intentioned people wanted to do *something* to improve the condition of Black undergraduate men on their campuses. In many instances, alarming statistics compelled them to act quickly and without serious strategic planning. As previously noted, older adults (usually faculty and staff) on many campuses were recruited and paired with Black undergraduate men, and mentoring was supposed to occur. Despite the popularity of mentoring programs, Harper (2012) reported the following from his study of 219 Black male college achievers at 42 colleges and universities:

> None said anything about their postsecondary institutions' structured mentoring programs as they named people, experiences, and resources that aided their college success. Put differently, no participant attributed even a fraction of his college achievement to a program that systematically matched him with faculty, staff, or peers with whom he was to routinely meet. (p. 16)

These programs and a range of other campus activities were hardly ever situated in a larger institutional strategy to improve Black male student success. Efforts were being launched in stand-alone and fragmented ways; they had not emerged from substantive, collaborative conversations and planning among cabinet-level leaders, academic deans and faculty, student affairs professionals, coaches and athletics administrators, and Black male students and alumni. Furthermore, a written strategy document that detailed a collective understanding of the institution's Black male student success problem was also missing on most campuses: What would be done, on what timeline, with what resources and by whom, and how would progress be measured? Instead, mentoring programs, 1- to 2-day summits, social activities, and Black male initiatives were being developed in the absence of standards such as those Harper and Kuykendall (2012) developed.

That the movement itself lacked strategy is noteworthy. Unlike K–12 school initiatives that have emerged from OSF's Campaign for Black Male Achievement, no one officially launched a movement focused on Black men in postsecondary education. Yet suddenly, dozens of articles started appearing in journals, books were being published, and professional conferences were abuzz with conversations about this population. It is possible that few people even recognized a movement had begun and was gaining momentum. It had no name, and there were no conveners, evaluators, or consortia of funders. People on college campuses across the country were unknowingly contributing to a directionless campaign.

Misplaced Onus for Student Success

Efforts born during the 15-year period tended to focus more on fixing the Black male student than on addressing structural and institutional forces that undermined his academic achievement, sense of belonging, and psychosocial development. Teaching him how to survive in racist classroom environments, for example, was often chosen over educating professors about the ways their pedagogical practices and other actions sustained racism and the marginalization of Black men in courses they taught. Concerning student engagement, one question was repeatedly asked by researchers and professionals alike: Why are Black men so disengaged? Insights into what faculty members and student affairs professionals were doing to engage these undergraduates in enriching educational experiences, inside and outside the classroom, were not how most conversations related to student engagement were framed.

Like many other diversity problems on predominantly White college campuses, the work of addressing troubling trends among Black male students usually fell on chief diversity officers, directors of Black cultural centers and multicultural affairs offices, or on a particular person of color in the student affairs division. Academic schools and departments were uncommon sites for institutional activity. Presidents, provosts, deans, academic department chairs, tenured professors, and high-ranking others typically were not at the table when important conversations were taking place about the status of Black men on campus. Likewise, as Harper and Harris (2012) note, policymakers had no real role in the movement. Consequently, insufficient programming in disjointed campus corners occurred in lieu of structural and macrolevel changes.

Amplification of Deficits

"Two-thirds who start college do not graduate within six years" and "they are among the most disengaged students on college campuses" (Harper, 2012; Harper & Harris, 2012) are just two of many trends repeatedly emphasized in academic publications, newspaper and magazine articles, and conference presentations pertaining to Black male undergraduates. The near-exclusive focus on problems plaguing this population inadvertently reinforced a hopeless, deficit-oriented narrative. Interventions introduced during the 15-year period were based almost entirely on bad data, statistical and observational reports of bad behaviors and outcomes, especially in comparison to other groups (Black women, White undergraduate men, etc.). Well-intentioned educators and researchers invested disproportionate energies into investigating the explanatory undercurrents of Black men's stagnant enrollments and other troubling outcomes. Doing so was critically important, as new insights helped justify the creation of many institutional activities described earlier in this chapter.

Few initiatives were grounded in data and perspectives gathered from Black male achievers. Take, for example, the college completion statistic. Almost all the attention was placed on the two-thirds who did not complete college instead of trying to understand which personal and institutional factors helped one-third persist through baccalaureate degree attainment. Harper (2012) reports the following from the National Black Male College Achievement Study:

> Most surprising and most disappointing is that nearly every student interviewed said it was the first time someone had sat him down to ask how he successfully navigated his way to and through higher education, what compelled him to be engaged in student organizations and college classrooms, and what he learned that could help improve achievement and engagement among Black male collegians. (p. 15)

Harper further notes that 219 of 221 invited students agreed to participate in a 2- to 3-hour interview focused on their success, which suggests that Black men who do well in college are willing to share their navigational strategies and identify conditions that bolster their success. Unfortunately, education professionals, researchers, and journalists rarely sought them out. Therefore, interventions created to improve Black male student achievement were informed almost entirely by Black male students who did not succeed in college.

Men Without Masculinities

A small number of studies published during the 15-year period (e.g., Dancy, 2011, 2012; Harper, 2004; Harris et al., 2011; Martin & Harris, 2006) focused explicitly on masculinities and gender performativity among Black undergraduate men. Theories and frameworks from psychology, sociology, and gender or men's studies that help explain precollege gender socialization, poor trends in seeking help, gender role conflicts, and masculine expression anxieties among college-age men informed the conceptual design of these studies and the interpretation of data collected. Conversations at conferences and 1- to 2-day summits were hardly ever about masculinities among Black undergraduate men. Instead, the emphasis was on enrollment, engagement, and completion trends, with little to no consideration of how troubled masculinities may have contributed to any of these factors.

Masculinities were also mishandled in many Black male initiatives created during the movement. Like the conversations at conferences and summits, programs and activities emerging from these initiatives focused mostly on strengthening unity and social satisfaction among Black undergraduate men, offering them restorative shelters from alienating predominantly White campus spaces, centralizing resources for their academic survival and success, and facilitating opportunities for their leadership development. Often missing were opportunities for them to critically reflect on themselves as men and acquire the tools necessary for disrupting patriarchy, sexism, misogyny, and homophobia within Black communities. The emphasis was primarily (sometimes exclusively) on increasing the number of Black male college graduates, without devoting much attention to their development into healthy and productive people who would eventually become spouses, partners, and fathers. Attempting to improve rates of success among these young men without paying sufficient attention to important (and sometimes conflict-laden) aspects of their masculinities was surely shortsighted.

Homogenization of Black Undergraduate Men

"Which Black men?" is not a question that seems to have been carefully contemplated in the design and implementation of many Black male initiatives and campus activities. Harper and Nichols (2008) identified tremendous in-group diversity among Black undergraduate men at the three institutions in their study. Substantive differences in their socioeconomic backgrounds, geographic and community origins (urban versus rural), sexual orientation, and group affiliations (student athletes, fraternity members, Black student union leaders, etc.) affected their interactions and solidarity, often in problematic ways. Moreover, Massey, Mooney, Torres, and Charles (2007) highlighted differences in the social origins of Black immigrant and Black American students at highly selective colleges and universities. These and other differences often went unacknowledged among panelists at Black male summits, authors of peer-reviewed studies, and architects of campus programming. Consequently, efforts intended to reach Black men inadvertently excluded particular subgroups within the race. Targeted, differentiated outreach to diverse sectors of Black male students was atypical; hence, attendance and participation rates in campus initiatives were often much lower than desired.

The homogenization of Black men was also evident in the substance of campus initiatives; race and being Black was foremost. As previously mentioned, the focus was rarely on Black male students as gendered beings. Furthermore, the ways race and gender intersected with other dimensions of their identities (e.g., sexual orientations, [dis]ability, spirituality and religiosity, and socioeconomic status) were often not thoughtfully considered. It is quite possible that gay and bisexual men felt marginalized and excluded as their sexualities went unacknowledged. This was likely exacerbated in social spaces where Black male students were discussing romantic and sexual pursuits in exclusively heterosexist ways, or in leadership development programs that emphasized "acceptable" forms of masculine self-presentation. Another example is Black male retreats that included rites of passage rituals that reinforced patriarchal and hypermasculine notions of Black male leadership; effeminate men or those who did not perform their masculinities in a manner that has been socially constructed as strong probably experienced dissonance and alienation.

Small-Sample, Student-Exclusive, Single-Site Studies

As noted previously in this chapter, more than 60 peer-reviewed studies pertaining to Black male collegians were published in academic journals between 1997 and 2012. Despite this knowledge production, institutional leaders and faculty members as well as policymakers continually sustain practices, environmental conditions, and policies that cyclically undermine Black male student success. This could be attributable, at least in part, to the narrow methodological scope of research published during this era. Like many articles listed in Table 5.2, the overwhelming majority of studies on Black undergraduate men is based on samples with an average of 27 participants on a single college campus. Quantitative and large-scale, multisite qualitative studies have been in short supply. Therefore, findings and recommendations emerging from them tend to be context-bound and understandably interpreted with suspicion; most are far from generalizable.

While qualitative studies that provide nuanced understandings of a small number of students' experiences have considerable value, those tend not to offer sufficient cross-sectional insights to ignite institutional change and policy formation. Thick, rich, descriptive accounts that explain various phenomena are important and necessary, but so too are research studies that are big enough to influence macrolevel decision making in higher education. The popularity of studies based on onetime short interviews at a single institution raises at least one question about the goals of scholars who produced them: Were we writing for the sake of publication productivity (numbers), mere consciousness-raising and perhaps professional advancement (promotion and tenure), or were we writing to influence structural change on behalf of a population commonly underserved on college campuses? If it was the latter, then methods employed in most studies published during the 15-year period contradict our aims.

Another shortcoming of the existing published scholarship is that students have almost always been the sole unit of analysis in research studies. Data were rarely collected from administrators and faculty; policies affecting Black male college access and achievement were not analyzed with any degree of regularity. Moreover, ethnographic studies that entail extended fieldwork (e.g., 12 months on a campus) and systematic observations of students' interactions with various institutional actors and structures have been unpopular; instead, interviewing a few students once for 30 to 90 minutes has been more common. No national, cross-sectional quantitative study of Black undergraduate men and the characteristics of institutions where they were enrolled was launched during the 15-year period.

Moving Black Women to the Margins: Another Unintended Consequence

Quantifiable differences between Black undergraduate men and their same-race female peers were used to justify the creation of male-exclusive initiatives created between 1997 and 2012. During this era, considerably more Black women than Black men applied to and enrolled in postsecondary institutions. Black undergraduates in 1980 consisted of 57.9 percent women, compared to 63.1 percent in 2011 (U.S. Department of Education, 2013). Hence, the sex gap in enrollments has increased over time. These differences are more severe in particular sectors of higher education. At some HBCUs, for example, Black women outnumber their male counterparts by rates of 3 to 1. Lundy-Wagner and Gasman (2011) show the general consistency of this trend over time, which led to this conclusion: "The African American enrollment gap favoring women at HBCUs is not new. African American men *may* have only outnumbered women at HBCUs from their inception to the mid-1920s" (p. 947). Notwithstanding these historical patterns, scholars, campus leaders, and others seem to have become more troubled by the recent widening sex gap in enrollment, which ultimately produced alarming differences in Black students' degree attainment rates.

As shown in Figure 5.1, men earned roughly one-third of the degrees awarded to Black students across all levels, from associate through doctoral. Harper et al.'s (2013) analyses of six-year student athlete graduation rates across 76 universities in the six major intercollegiate sports conferences revealed an interesting set of trends among Black students. Specifically, at many institutions Black women graduated at higher rates than did most other groups of student athletes, including their White female teammates. For instance, in the Southeastern Conference, Black female student athletes' average six-year graduation rate (across four cohorts) was 74.6 percent, compared to 72.9 percent for White female student-athletes and 68.5 percent for undergraduate students overall on the 14 campuses. Comparatively, only 45.4 percent of Black male student athletes at those universities completed baccalaureate degree programs within six years.

FIGURE 5.1 Black Student Postsecondary Degree Attainment by Level and Sex, 2011

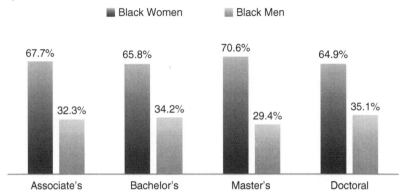

Note. Authors' calculations using data from *Digest of Education Statistics, 2012*, by U.S. Department of Education, 2013, Washington, DC: Institute of Education Sciences, National Center for Education Statistics.

In addition to sex gaps in enrollment and attainment, documented and observed differences in Black student engagement added further justification for the investment of institutional resources in male initiatives. Based on data collected from 6,765 Black student respondents to the College Student Experiences Questionnaire, Cuyjet (1997) found that men devoted less time to studying, took notes in class less often, spent significantly less time writing and revising papers, and participated less often in class-related collaborative experiences than female respondents to the survey. Furthermore, Black women were more engaged in campus activities, looked more frequently in their campus newspapers for notices about upcoming events and engagement opportunities, attended more meetings and programs, served on more campus committees, and held more leadership positions at their institutions.

Similarly, Harper, Carini, Bridges, and Hayek's (2004) analysis of data collected from 1,167 Black undergraduates at 12 HBCUs participating in the National Survey of Student Engagement revealed statistically significant differences between men and women in activities such as studying, reading, preparing for class, writing papers, and working hard to meet professors' expectations. Black male HBCU students were less engaged than their female counterparts in these academic endeavors. As one measure of engagement, 57 percent of Black female respondents to the Community College Survey of Student Engagement (2005), compared to 45 percent of Black male respondents, indicated that they often or very often discussed readings and course content with others outside of class. Professionals and administrators from a wide range of institution types were reporting similar engagement norms at national conferences and elsewhere during the 15-year period.

Sex differences in student engagement help explain, at least in part, academic performance gaps between Black male and female undergraduates. At summits and national conferences there were numerous anecdotal reports of Black men earning the lowest grade point averages (GPAs) among all undergraduates on a particular campus. Analyses of GPAs, disaggregated by sex, were not furnished in studies published between 1997 and 2012. This is likely attributable to the confidentiality of students' academic records and the sensitivity of academic performance data. Table 5.5 shows sex differences in GPAs among undergraduate members of the nine national historically Black Greek-letter organizations at a dozen large predominantly White public universities. Accordingly, during the 2011–2012 academic school year Black female members, on average, maintained a 3.02 cumulative GPA, compared to 2.67 for Black fraternity men. It is noteworthy that each of these national sororities and fraternities espouses a commitment to academic excellence in its mission statement, and has a minimum GPA requirement to join.

Trends such as these have helped manufacture an erroneous presumption that now permeates American higher education: that everything is just fine with Black female collegians. Statistical indicators were used as rationale for a 15-year-long focus on Black male students. Little about Black undergraduate women was published, few 1- to 2-day campus summits pertaining to their needs and issues were held, comprehensive Black female initiatives were not created, and they were rarely the topic of discussion at national higher education conferences. Black women's experiential realities were overshadowed by their statistical comparisons to Black men. They, too, grapple with many of the problems identified in Harper (2013): onlyness (the experience of being the only or one of only a few non-White students in a college classroom), niggering (stereotypes, racial microaggressions, and racist misconceptions regarding their intellectual competence and belongingness), and the shortage of same-race faculty role models on predominantly White campuses. Additionally, racism and sexism converge for them in unique ways that are psychologically and academically poisonous. They routinely outperformed their same-race male counterparts but often fell beneath women from other racial groups and White men on most measures of success. Despite this, the gender-exclusive 15-year movement pushed Black women's issues to the margins. It could be reasonably argued that higher education scholars, administrators, journalists, and others, perhaps unintentionally, left Black female undergraduates behind during this era.

TABLE 5.5
Black Sorority and Fraternity Members' GPAs, 2011–2012

Institution	Sororities	Fraternities
Auburn University	2.89	2.50
Clemson University	3.04	2.94
Florida State University	3.09	2.62
Georgia Institute of Technology	3.20	2.88
North Carolina State University	2.84	2.80
Ohio State University	3.11	2.68
Purdue University	3.14	2.63
University of Florida	3.12	2.87
University of Missouri	2.78	2.04
University of North Carolina at Chapel Hill	2.92	2.75
University of South Carolina	3.02	2.72
Virginia Polytechnic Institute and State University	3.13	2.60

Note. From "Greek Life Statistics," Auburn University Greek Life, 2012, https://cws.auburn. edu/studentAffairs/greekLife/statistics.aspx; "Policies, Grades and Statistics," Clemson University Campus Life, 2013, www.clemson.edu/campus-life/fraternity-sorority-life/grades-stats .html; "Scholarship Reports," Florida State University Office of Greek Life, 2013, http://greek life.fsu.edu/Dates-Resources/Scholarship-Reports; "Greek Affairs: Reports," Georgia Tech Dean of Students, 2013, www.greek.gatech.edu/plugins/content/index.php?id=4; "Reports: Grades & Membership," North Carolina State University Greek Life, 2013, www.ncsu.edu/greeklife/ reports.php; "Ohio Union: Grade reports," The Ohio State University, 2013, http://ohiounion .osu.edu/get_involved/sorority_fraternity/grade_reports; "Purdue Greeks," Purdue Fraternity and Sorority Life, n.d., www.purduegreeks.com/#_p.Resources%2FGrade%20Reports; "Sorority & Fraternity Affairs: Grade Reports," University of Florida Student Activities and Involvement, 2013, www.studentinvolvement.ufl.edu/SororityFraternityAffairs/Resources/ GradeReports; "Grades: Chapter Academic Records," University of Missouri Office of Greek Life, 2012, http://greeklife.missouri.edu/greek-statistics/greek-statistics/; "Academic Reports," University of North Carolina at Chapel Hill Fraternity & Sorority Life and Community Involvement, n.d., http://ofslci.unc.edu/greeks/reports; "Fraternity and Sorority Report, Fall 2012," University of South Carolina, 2013, www.sa.sc.edu/fsl/files/2010/10/Greek -Report-Fall-2012-FINAL.pdf; "Fraternity and Sorority Life: Academic Reports," Virginia Tech Division of Student Affairs, 2013, www.greeklife.vt.edu/resources/academicreports .html.

Improving Success for College Men of Color: A Better Way Forward

The 15-year movement to improve Black male student success was not a complete failure. Among its most praiseworthy accomplishments is the national conversation it ignited. Undoubtedly, more people within and outside higher education are more aware of the troubling status of these students than they were prior to 1997. In some ways, the movement is also a promising example of the momentum that could be created across hundreds (perhaps thousands) of college and university campuses in response to a set of pressing issues plaguing a particular population. The attention devoted to Black men has been remarkable. Nevertheless, problematic features of the movement must be corrected. This is especially important as a broader, more inclusive agenda is being crafted for college men of color.

Future institutional responses to challenges that undermine access, engagement, academic achievement, psychosocial development, and attainment for AAPI, Black, Latino, and Native American men must be strategic. Assuming greater institutional responsibility for the success of these students is a requisite first step that entails bringing together stakeholders from all corners and levels of the institution—from the president and provost to tenured professors, student affairs professionals, and undergraduate students—to study these problems in systematic ways, collaboratively develop plans of action that include classroom and out-of-class interventions, and devise assessment and accountability mechanisms to ensure the institution reaches its student success goals. Questions such as, "Why do so few Black men apply to this college?" must be replaced with critical examinations of how and why the institution fails to attract more Black male applicants. Metrics such as those developed by Harper and Kuykendall (2012) also would be useful. Examples of five campuses that adopted these standards, created cross-sectional teams, and assumed institutional responsibility for Black male student achievement are provided in Harper's (2014) report.

To ensure success for college men of color, anti-deficit perspectives should inform future initiatives created for them. Commonly asked questions such as, "Why are they so disengaged?" for example, must be replaced with inquiries regarding the impetus for engagement among those who participate actively in their classes, study in disciplined ways, collaborate frequently on academic matters with peers outside of class, participate actively in a variety of clubs and organizations, and take advantage of enriching educational experiences (study abroad programs, summer internships related to their majors, collaborative research opportunities with faculty, etc.). Harper's (2012) anti-deficit achievement framework in Figure 5.2 includes several

FIGURE 5.2 Anti-Deficit Achievement Framework

PRE-COLLEGE SOCIALIZATION AND READINESS	COLLEGE ACHIEVEMENT		POST-COLLEGE SUCCESS

COLLEGE ACHIEVEMENT

POST-COLLEGE SUCCESS

GRADUATE SCHOOL ENROLLMENT

What happened in college to develop and support Black male students' interest in pursuing degrees beyond the baccalaureate?

How do Black undergraduate men who experience racism at predominantly White universities maintain their commitment to pursuing graduate and professional degrees at similar types of institutions?

CLASSROOM EXPERIENCES

Which instructional practices best engage Black male collegians?

How do Black men craft productive responses to stereotypes encountered in classrooms?

CAREER READINESS

Which college experiences enable Black men to compete successfully for careers in their fields?

What prepares Black male achievers for the racial politics they will encounter in post-college workplace settings?

How do faculty and other institutional agents enhance Black men's career development and readiness?

FACULTY

PERSISTENCE

PEERS

ENRICHING EDUCATIONAL EXPERIENCES

What developmental gains do Black male achievers attribute to studying abroad?

How do Black men cultivate value-added relationships with faculty and administrators?

What do Black male students find appealing about doing research with professors?

FAMILIAL FACTOR

How do family members nurture and sustain Black male students' interest in school?

How do parents help shape Black men's college aspirations?

What compels one to speak and participate actively in courses in which he is the only Black student?

How do Black undergraduate men earn GPAs above 3.0 in majors for which they were academically underprepared?

OUT-OF-CLASS ENGAGEMENT

What compels Black men to take advantage of campus resources and engagement opportunities?

What unique educational benefits and outcomes are conferred to Black male student leaders?

How do achievers foster mutually supportive relationships with their lower-performing same-race male peers?

K-12 SCHOOL FORCES

What do teachers and other school agents do to assist Black men in getting to college?

How do Black male students negotiate academic achievement alongside peer acceptance?

OUT-OF-SCHOOL PREP RESOURCES

How do low-income and first generation Black male students acquire knowledge about college?

Which programs and experiences enhance Black men's college readiness?

Note. From *Black Male Student Success in Higher Education: A Report from the National Black Male College Achievement Study*, p. 5, by S. R. Harper, 2012, Philadelphia: University of Pennsylvania, Center for the Study of Race and Equity in Education. Copyright 2014 by the Trustees of the University of Pennsylvania. Redrawn with permission.

examples of how questions commonly asked about failure, disengagement, insufficiency, and underperformance can be inverted to ascertain instructive insights into student achievement.

As previously mentioned, more has been written about Black undergraduate men over the past 15 years than the three other men-of-color groups combined. Additional scholarship has to be produced to provide a more nuanced understanding of Native American, Latino, and AAPI men's experiences and outcomes in postsecondary educational contexts. This research, as well as future studies on Black undergraduate men, must be methodologically sophisticated and based on more institutions and larger student samples. This is not to suggest that rich, deeply textured small qualitative studies are no longer useful. They add considerable value to our understanding of who students are and how they experience higher education. But macrolevel institutional and policy change is unlikely to ensue in the absence of studies that reach further and include more participants.

Researchers and education professionals alike must pay more careful attention to in-group diversity as they study college men of color and create initiatives that attempt to respond to their varied needs. This is especially critical among AAPI and Latino men, as there are substantive dissimilarities across ethnic/cultural subgroups. The same can be said for tribal differences among Native American male students. Any effort to appeal generally to men of color or even to one particular broad racial group will inevitably fall short of attracting all male students therein. Hence, it must be multipronged, as well as marketed and delivered in ways that account for students with intersecting identities (e.g., low-income Pacific Islanders, gay Native American men, and Latino atheists).

Moving forward, architects of men-of-color campus initiatives must be mindful of the masculinities students enter college with, as well as how they develop, negotiate, and perform their gender identities on campus. Programming and other interventions (e.g., one-on-one advising with students) should aim to unmask and address the sociological undercurrents of men's bad behaviors and poor help-seeking tendencies. Likewise, spaces should be created that offer men opportunities to engage in critical individual and collective reflection on how they have been socialized to think of themselves as men; the origins of their sexist and misogynistic perspectives on women; how and why they embrace homophobia; how patriarchy and heterosexism undermine solidarity in communities of color; and what kinds of partners or spouses, fathers, and citizens they aspire to be in their postcollege lives. Increasing enrollments and completion rates among college men of color should remain among the highest priorities of campus initiatives, but graduating well-developed men with strong, conflict-free gender identities must also be of the utmost importance.

Finally, efforts enacted to improve the status of Latino, Native American, AAPI, and Black male students should not be at the expense of women of color. While statistics often indicate they are doing comparatively better, undergraduate women have developmental needs and face a range of gender-specific challenges that deserve resources and attention. Scholars and various institutional agents need to invest more energy in understanding the unique gendered experiences of women and men of color on campus. These understandings should lead to actions and activities that are sometimes, but not always, tailored along gender-exclusive lines. Understanding their experiences can prevent a repetition of the marginalization of women that occurred during the 15-year movement to improve Black male student success in higher education.

References

Auburn University Greek Life. (2012). *Greek life statistics.* Retrieved October 19, 2013, from https://cws.auburn.edu/studentAffairs/greekLife/statistics.aspx

Beamon, K. K., & Bell, P. A. (2006). Academics versus athletics: An examination of the effects of background and socialization on African American male student athletes. *Social Science Journal, 43*(3), 393–403.

Benson, K. F. (2000). Constructing academic inadequacy: African American athletes' stories of schooling. *The Journal of Higher Education, 71*(2), 223–246.

Bonner, F. A., II. (2003). To be young, gifted, African American, and male. *Gifted Child Today, 26*(2), 26–34.

Bonner, F. A., II. (2010). Academically gifted African American male college students. Santa Barbara, CA: Praeger.

Brown, A. L. (2011). "Same old stories": The Black male in social science and educational literature, 1930s to the present. *Teacher College Record, 113*(9), 2047–2079.

Brown, M. C., II, Dancy, T. E., II, & Davis, J. E. (Eds.). (2013). *Educating African American males: Contexts for consideration, possibilities for practice.* New York, NY: Peter Lang.

Byrne, D. N. (Ed.). (2006). *HBCU's models for success: Supporting achievement and retention of Black males.* New York, NY: Thurgood Marshall Scholarship Fund.

Clemson University Campus Life. (2013). *Policies, grades and statistics.* Retrieved October 19, 2013, from http://www.clemson.edu/campus-life/fraternity-sorority-life/grades-stats.html

Community College Survey of Student Engagement. (2005). *Engaging students, challenging the odds: 2005 findings.* Austin: University of Texas Press.

Cuyjet, M. J. (Ed.). (1997). Helping African American men succeed in college. *New Directions for Student Services, 80.* San Francisco, CA: Jossey-Bass.

Cuyjet, M. J. (Ed.). (2006). *African American men in college.* San Francisco, CA: Jossey-Bass.

Dancy, T. E., II. (2011). Colleges in the making of manhood and masculinity: Gendered perspectives on African American males. *Gender and Education*, *23*(4), 477–495.

Dancy, T. E., II. (2012). *The brother code: Manhood and masculinity among African American males in college*. Charlotte, NC: Information Age.

Dancy, T. E., II, & Brown, M. C., II. (2008). Unintended consequences: African American male educational attainment and collegiate perceptions after Brown v. Board of Education. *American Behavioral Scientist*, *51*(7), 984–1003.

Dancy, T. E., II, & Brown, M. C., II (Eds.). (2012). *African American males and education: Researching the convergence of race and identity*. Charlotte, NC: Information Age.

Eckholm, E. (2006, March 20). Plight deepens for Black men, studies warn. *The New York Times*. Retrieved November 13, 2013, from http://www.nytimes.com/2006/03/20/national/20blackmen.html?pagewanted=all&_r=0

Florida State University Office of Greek Life. (2013). *Scholarship reports*. Retrieved October 19, 2013, from http://greeklife.fsu.edu/Dates-Resources/Scholarship-Reports

Frierson, H. T., Pearson, W., Jr., & Wyche, J. H. (Eds.). (2009). *Black American males in higher education: Diminishing proportions*. Bingley, UK: Emerald Group.

Frierson, H. T., Wyche, J. H., & Pearson, W., Jr. (Eds.). (2009). *Black American males in higher education: Research, programs and academe*. Bingley, UK: Emerald Group.

Georgia Tech Dean of Students. (2013). *Greek affairs: Reports*. Retrieved October 19, 2013, from http://www.greek.gatech.edu/plugins/content/index.php?id=4

Glenn, F. S. (2004). The retention of Black male students in Texas public community colleges. *Journal of College Student Retention: Research, Theory & Practice*, *5*(2), 115–133.

Goode-Cross, D. T., & Good, G. E. (2009). Managing multiple-minority identities: African American men who have sex with men at predominately White universities. *Journal of Diversity in Higher Education*, *2*(2), 103–112.

Goode-Cross, D. T., & Tager, D. (2011). Negotiating multiple identities: How African American gay and bisexual men persist at a predominantly White institution. *Journal of Homosexuality*, *58*(9), 1235–1254.

Gordon, E. T., Gordon, E. W., & Nembhard, J. G. G. (1994). Social science literature concerning African American men. *The Journal of Negro Education*, *63*(4), 508–531.

Hagedorn, L. S., Maxwell, W., & Hampton, P. (2002). Correlates of retention for African American males in community colleges. *Journal of College Student Retention*, *3*(3), 243–263.

Harper, S. R. (2004). The measure of a man: Conceptualizations of masculinity among high-achieving African American male college students. *Berkeley Journal of Sociology*, *48*(1), 89–107.

Harper, S. R. (2006). *Black male students at public universities in the U.S.: Status, trends and implications for policy and practice*. Washington, DC: Joint Center for Political and Economic Studies.

Harper, S. R. (2009). Niggers no more: A critical race counternarrative on Black male student achievement at predominantly White colleges and universities. *International Journal of Qualitative Studies in Education, 22*(6), 697–712.

Harper, S. R. (2012). *Black male student success in higher education: A report from the national Black male college achievement study.* Philadelphia: University of Pennsylvania, Center for the Study of Race and Equity in Education.

Harper, S. R. (2013). Am I my brother's teacher? Black undergraduates, peer pedagogies, and racial socialization in predominantly White postsecondary contexts. *Review of Research in Education, 37*(1), 183–211.

Harper, S. R. (2014). *Institutional responsibility for Black male student success: What five colleges and universities are doing to improve Black undergraduate men's experiences and outcomes.* Philadelphia: University of Pennsylvania, Center for the Study of Race and Equity in Education.

Harper, S. R., & Associates. (in press). *Succeeding in the city: A report from the New York City Black and Latino Male High School Achievement Study.* Philadelphia: University of Pennsylvania, Center for the Study of Race and Equity in Education.

Harper, S. R., Carini, R. M., Bridges, B. K., & Hayek, J. C. (2004). Gender differences in student engagement among African American undergraduates at historically Black colleges and universities. *Journal of College Student Development, 45*(3), 271–284.

Harper, S. R., & Davis, C. H. F., III. (2012). They (don't) care about education: A counternarrative on Black male students' responses to inequitable schooling. *Educational Foundations, 26*(1), 103–120.

Harper, S. R., Davis, R. J., Jones, D. E., McGowan, B. L., Ingram, T. N., & Platt, C. S. (2011). Race and racism in the experiences of Black male resident assistants at predominantly White universities. *Journal of College Student Development, 52*(2), 180–200.

Harper, S. R., & Gasman, M. (2008). Consequences of conservatism: Black male students and the politics of historically Black colleges and universities. *The Journal of Negro Education, 77*(4), 336–351.

Harper, S. R., & Harris, F., III. (2012). *A role for policymakers in improving the status of Black male students in U.S. higher education.* Washington, DC: Institute for Higher Education Policy.

Harper, S. R., & Kuykendall, J. A. (2012). Institutional efforts to improve Black male student achievement: A standards-based approach. *Change, 44*(2), 23–29.

Harper, S. R., & Nichols, A. H. (2008). Are they not all the same? Racial heterogeneity among Black male undergraduates. *Journal of College Student Development, 49*(3), 247–269.

Harper, S. R., & Quaye, S. J. (2007). Student organizations as venues for Black identity expression and development among African American male student leaders. *Journal of College Student Development, 48*(2), 127–144.

Harper, S. R., Williams, C. D., Jr., & Blackman, H. W. (2013). *Black male student-athletes and racial inequities in NCAA Division I college sports.* Philadelphia: University of Pennsylvania, Center for the Study of Race and Equity in Education.

Harris, F., III, Palmer, R. T., & Struve, L. E. (2011). "Cool posing" on campus: A qualitative study of masculinities and gender expression among Black men at a private research institution. *The Journal of Negro Education, 80*(1), 47–62.

Hilton, A. A., Wood, J. L., & Lewis, C. W. (Eds.). (2012). *Black males in postsecondary education: Examining their experiences in diverse institutional contexts.* Charlotte, NC: Information Age.

Jackson, B. A. (2012). Bonds of brotherhood: Emotional and social support among college Black men. *ANNALS of the American Academy of Political and Social Science, 642*(1), 61–71.

Jackson, J. F. L., & Moore, J. L., III. (2008). The African American male crisis in education: A popular media infatuation or needed public policy response? *American Behavioral Scientist, 51*(7), 847–853.

Jones, R. L. (2004). *Black haze: Violence, sacrifice, and manhood in Black Greek-letter fraternities.* Albany, NY: SUNY Press.

Lewis, S., Simon, C., Uzzell, R., Horwitz, A., & Casserly, M. (2010). *A call for change: The social and educational factors contributing to the outcomes of Black males in urban schools.* Washington, DC: Council of the Great City Schools.

Lundy-Wagner, V., & Gasman, M. (2011). When gender issues are not just about women: Reconsidering male students at historically Black colleges and universities. *Teachers College Record, 113*(5), 934–968.

Martin, B. E., & Harris, F., III. (2006). Examining productive conceptions of masculinities: Lessons learned from academically driven African American male student-athletes. *The Journal of Men's Studies, 14*(3), 359–378.

Massey, D. S., Mooney, M., Torres, K. C., & Charles, C. Z. (2007). Black immigrants and Black natives attending selective colleges and universities in the United States. *American Journal of Education, 113*(2), 243–271.

North Carolina State University Greek Life. (2013). *Reports: Grades & membership.* Retrieved October 19, 2013, from http://www.ncsu.edu/greeklife/reports.php

The Ohio State University. (2013). *Ohio Union: Grade reports.* Retrieved October 19, 2013, from http://ohiounion.osu.edu/get_involved/sorority_fraternity/grade_reports

Oseguera, L. (2010). Success despite the image: How African American male student-athletes endure their academic journey amidst negative characterizations. *Journal for the Study of Sports and Athletes in Education, 4*(3), 297–324.

Palmer, R. T., Davis, R. J., & Hilton, A. A. (2009). Exploring challenges that threaten to impede the academic success of academically underprepared Black males at an HBCU. *Journal of College Student Development, 50*(4), 429–445.

Palmer, R. T., & Wood, J. L. (Eds.). (2012). *Black men in college: Implications for HBCUs and beyond.* New York, NY: Routledge.

Patton, L. D. (2011). Perspectives on identity, disclosure, and the campus environment among African American gay and bisexual men at one historically Black college. *Journal of College Student Development, 52*(1), 77–100.

Polite, V. C., & Davis, J. E. (Eds.). (1999). *African American males in school and society: Practices and policies for effective education.* New York, NY: Teachers College Press.

Purdue Fraternity and Sorority Life. (n.d.). *Purdue Greeks*. Retrieved October 19, 2013, from http://www.purduegreeks.com/#_p.Resources%2FGrade%20 Reports

Riggins, R. K., McNeal, C., & Herndon, M. K. (2008). The role of spirituality among African-American college males attending a historically Black university. *College Student Journal, 42*(1), 70–81.

Roach, R. (2001). Where are the Black men on campus? *Black Issues in Higher Education, 18*(6), 18–21.

Rodney, H. E., Tachia, H. R., & Rodney, L. W. (1997). The effect of family and social support on feelings and past acts of violence among African American college men. *Journal of American College Health, 46*(3), 103–108.

Ross, M. J. (1998). *Success factors of young African American males at a historically Black college*. New York, NY: Praeger.

Schott Foundation for Public Education. (2010). *Yes we can: The Schott 50 state report on public education and Black males*. Cambridge, MA: Author.

Shah, S., & Sato, G. (2012). *Where do we go from here? Philanthropic support for Black men and boys*. New York, NY: Foundation Center.

Sellers, R. M., & Kuperminc, G. P. (1997). Goal discrepancy in African American male student-athletes' unrealistic expectations for careers in professional sports. *Journal of Black Psychology, 23*(1), 6–23.

Singer, J. N. (2005). Understanding racism through the eyes of African American male student-athletes. *Race Ethnicity and Education, 8*(4), 365–386.

Smith, W. A., Allen, W. R., & Danley, L. L. (2007). Assume the position . . . you fit the description: Psychosocial experiences and racial battle fatigue among African American male college students. *American Behavioral Scientist, 51*(4), 551–578.

Strayhorn, T. L. (2008a). Fittin' in: Do diverse interactions with peers affect sense of belonging for Black men at predominantly White institutions? *Journal of Student Affairs Research and Practice, 45*(4), 953–979.

Strayhorn, T. L. (2008b). The role of supportive relationships in facilitating African American males' success in college. *Journal of Student Affairs Research and Practice, 45*(1), 26–48.

Strayhorn, T. L., Blakewood, A. M., & DeVita, J. M. (2008). Factors affecting the college choice of African American gay male undergraduates: Implications for retention. *National Association of Student Affairs Professionals Journal, 11*(1), 88–108.

Strayhorn, T. L., & Mullins, T. G. (2012). Investigating Black gay male undergraduates' experiences in campus residence halls. *Journal of College and University Student Housing, 39*(1), 140–161.

Toldson, I. A. (2008). *Breaking barriers: Plotting the path to academic success for school-age African-American males*. Washington, DC: Congressional Black Caucus Foundation.

Toldson, I. A. (2011). *Breaking barriers 2: Plotting the path away from juvenile detention and toward academic success for school-age African American males*. Washington, DC: Congressional Black Caucus Foundation.

Toldson, I. A., & Lewis, C. W. (2012). *Challenge the status quo: Academic success among school-age African-American males.* Washington, DC: Congressional Black Caucus Foundation.

University of Florida Student Activities and Involvement. (2013). *Sorority & fraternity affairs: Grade reports.* Retrieved October 19, 2013, from https://www.studentinvolvement.ufl.edu/SororityFraternityAffairs/Resources/GradeReports

University of Missouri Office of Greek Life. (2012). *Grades: Chapter academic records.* Retrieved October 19, 2013, from http://greeklife.missouri.edu/greek-statistics/greek-statistics

University of North Carolina at Chapel Hill Fraternity & Sorority Life and Community Involvement. (n.d.). *Academic reports.* Retrieved October 19, 2013, from http://ofslci.unc.edu/greeks/reports

University of South Carolina. (2013). *Fraternity and sorority report, fall 2012.* Retrieved October 19, 2013, from http://www.sa.sc.edu/fsl/files/2010/10/Greek-Report-Fall-2012-FINAL.pdf

U.S. Department of Education. (2013). *Digest of education statistics, 2012.* Washington, DC: Institute of Education Sciences, National Center for Education Statistics.

Virginia Tech Division of Student Affairs. (2013). *Fraternity and sorority life: Academic reports.* Retrieved October 19, 2013, from http://www.greeklife.vt.edu/resources/academicreports.html

Washington, T. A., Wang, Y., & Browne, D. (2009). Difference in condom use among sexually active males at historically Black colleges and universities. *Journal of American College Health, 57*(4), 411–418.

Wood, J. L. (2012). Leaving the 2-year college: Predictors of Black male collegian departure. *Journal of Black Studies, 43*(3), 303–326.

Wood, J. L., Hilton, A. A., & Lewis, C. W. (2011). Black male collegians in public two-year colleges: Student perspectives on the effect of employment on academic success. *National Association of Student Affairs Professionals Journal, 14*(1), 97–110.

Wood, J. L., & Turner, C. S. (2011). Black males and the community college: Student perspectives on faculty and academic success. *Community College Journal of Research and Practice, 35*(1–2), 135–151.

Zamani-Gallaher, E. M., & Polite, V. C. (Eds.). (2010). *The state of the African American male.* East Lansing: Michigan State University Press.

CONTRIBUTORS

LeManuel Lee Bitsóí (Diné), Ed.D., currently serves as an associate in the Department of Organismic and Evolutionary Biology at Harvard University. In addition, Bitsóí is the lead Native American scholar for an initiative focusing on men of color sponsored by the College Board. As an advocate for minority scientists and scholars, Bitsóí also serves as the secretary for the board of directors for the Society for Advancement of Chicanos/Latinos and Native Americans in Science. Bitsóí previously served as the Diversity Action Plan Program director in the Department of Genetics at Harvard Medical School, and as training director for the FlyBase Model Organism Database in the Department of Molecular and Cellular Biology at Harvard, where he directed training programs for underrepresented minority students interested in pursuing genomic sciences at the undergraduate and postdoctoral levels.

Beth E. Bukoski, Ph.D., is an assistant professor at the University of Louisville in the Department of Leadership, Foundations, and Human Resource Education. She teaches courses on diversity, legal issues, the two-year college, and educational leadership. She is a qualitative and critical researcher, and her work centers on equity and diversity, particularly the experiences of underrepresented students and faculty as well as constructs of gender, sexuality, and race.

Edmund T. Gordon, Ph.D., is the chair of the African and African Diaspora Department as well as an associate professor in anthropology at the University of Texas at Austin. His teaching and research interests include culture and power in the African diaspora, gender studies (particularly Black males), critical race theory, race education, and the racial economy of space and resources. His publications include *Disparate Diasporas: Identity and Politics in an African-Nicaraguan Community* (Austin: University of Texas Press, 1998).

Shaun R. Harper, Ph.D., is on the faculty in the Graduate School of Education, Gender Studies, and Africana Studies at the University of Pennsylvania, where he also serves as director of the Center for the Study of Race and Equity in Education. Harper maintains an active research agenda that examines race and gender in higher education, Black male college access and achievement, and college student engagement. His 10 books include *Student Engagement in Higher Education* (New York, NY: Routledge, 2009), *College Men and Masculinities* (San Francisco, CA: Jossey-Bass, 2010), and the 5th edition of *Student Services: A Handbook for the Profession* (San Francisco, CA: Jossey-Bass, 2011).

Celeste Henery, Ph.D., is a postdoctoral fellow in the Department of African and African Diaspora Studies and the Institute for Policy Research and Analysis at the University of Texas at Austin. Her anthropological research has focused on issues of gendered Blackness and mental wellness in Brazil and the imaginative living of Black people across the diaspora.

Freeman A. Hrabowski III, Ph.D., has served as president of the University of Maryland, Baltimore County since 1992. His research and publications focus on science and math education, with a special emphasis on minority participation and performance. He chaired the National Academies' committee that investigated the underrepresentation of minorities in STEM disciplines. He also was named by President Barack Obama to chair the newly created President's Advisory Commission on Educational Excellence for African Americans. He has received numerous national and international honors, including being named one of the 100 Most Influential People in the World by *Time* magazine in 2012.

Lloyd L. Lee, Ph.D., is a citizen of the Navajo Nation. His clans are Kinyaa'áanii (Towering House) born for Tł'ááschíí (Red Bottom). His maternal grandfather clan is Áshįįhí (Salt) and his paternal grandfather clan is Tábąąhá (Water's Edge). He is assistant professor of Native American studies at the University of New Mexico in the Native American Studies department. He is director of the Institute of American Indian Research housed in the College of Arts and Sciences at the University of New Mexico. He also has been the book review editor for *American Indian Quarterly* for the past five years. He has published articles in *American Indian Quarterly*, *Wicazo Sa Review*, *AlterNative: An International Journal of Indigenous Peoples*, *International Journal of the Sociology of Language*, and *Indigenous Policy Journal*.

Loni Bordoloi Pazich is a Ph.D. candidate in higher and postsecondary education at the New York University Steinhardt School of Culture, Education, and Human Development. Her research focuses on the role of the state in facilitating equitable outcomes for students of color and immigrant students in higher education. She has served as a research associate at the

National Commission for Asian American and Pacific Islander Research in Education, the Texas Higher Education Coordinating Board, and the Center for Urban Education at the University of Southern California. Her work has appeared in *Educational Policy*.

Victor B. Sáenz, Ph.D., is an associate professor in the Department of Educational Administration at the University of Texas at Austin. He also holds a faculty appointment with the Center for Mexican American Studies and is a faculty fellow with the Division of Diversity and Community Engagement. His latest publications include an edited book, *Ensuring the Success of Latino Males in Higher Education: A New National Imperative* (Sterling, VA: Stylus, forthcoming, 2014), and a coauthored article in *Harvard Educational Review* focused on the coming home experience as a faculty member of color at the University of Texas at Austin.

Robert T. Teranishi, Ph.D., is the Morgan and Helen Chu Professor of Social Science, Comparative Education, and Asian American Studies at the University of California, Los Angeles. He is principal investigator for the National Commission on Asian American and Pacific Islander Research in Education. In 2011 Teranishi was appointed by Secretary of Education Arne Duncan to the U.S. Department of Education's Equity and Excellence Commission. He is the author of *Asians in the Ivory Tower: Dilemmas of Racial Inequality in American Higher Education* (New York, NY: Teachers College Press, 2011), which was honored with the Daniel E. Griffiths Research Award. His publications have appeared in numerous journals including *AAPI Nexus Journal, The Future of Children, Harvard Education Review, Harvard Kennedy School Asian American Policy Review, The Review of Higher Education,* and *Teachers College Record.*

Ronald A. Williams, Ph.D., is a former vice president of the College Board. Williams joined the College Board in 2007, after serving as president of Prince George's Community College in Largo, Maryland, since 1999. He currently chairs the National Society of Collegiate Scholars Community College Advisory Board and is a past member of the boards of the American Association of Colleges and Universities and the American Association of Community Colleges. Additionally, he is the past chair of the board of the Directorate for Education and Human Resources of the National Science Foundation. Williams has published three novels: *Four Saints and an Angel* (Pittsburgh, PA: Dorrance, 2009), *A Death in Panama* (Pittsburgh, PA: Dorrance, 2011), and *A Voice from the Tomb* (Pittsburgh, PA: Dorrance, 2013).

INDEX

AANAPISIs. *See* Asian American and Native American Pacific Islander-Serving Institutions

AAPI. *See* Asian American and Pacific Islander males

adolescence, study of men and, 97

African American youth, center-city, xi

Aid to Families with Dependent Children, 9

AIHEC. *See* American Indian Higher Education Consortium

American College Personnel Association, 118

American Indian Higher Education Consortium (AIHEC), 59, 74

American Indian Movement, 79n5

Anderson, Kim, 66, 70

Anthony, Susan B., 90

APIACU. *See* Asian Pacific Islander Association of Colleges and Universities

Arkansas African American Male Initiative, 125

Asian American and Native American Pacific Islander-Serving Institutions (AANAPISIs), 51

Asian American and Pacific Islander (AAPI) males, 35
  awareness raised regarding, 36
  challenges response for, 135
  college drop outs of, 44–45
  community of, 39
  convergence and, 38
  demographic characteristics of, 39–40
  disaggregated data collection for, 50
  educational attainment of, 38–39, 43–45
  educational mobility of, 41, 52
  gendered perspective on, 38
  heterogeneity in, 35
  inequity experienced by, 36
  intersectionality and, 35, 40–41
  as model minority, xv–xvi
  model minority myth and, 38, 49
  as monolithic and homogeneous whole, 39
  needs and challenges of, 41
  normative racial construction of, 37
  race and gender normative constructs and, 36–39
  refugee status of, 40
  research on, xv, 36, 117
  as research wedge group, 38
  secondary education level and, 41–43
  stereotypes of, 30n3
  unreliable data for population of, 40

Asian Pacific Islander Association of Colleges and Universities (APIACU), 51

autonomy theory, 92

Banks, Ralph Richard, 15

Barnhardt, R., 64

de Beauvoir, Simone, 90

Black culture, Moynihan report and, 19

Black feminism, 88, 94–95
  intersectional feminist theory and, 6
  patriarchy and, 5–6

Black Issues in Higher Education, 117

Black male crisis
  categories for, 21
  matriarchal structure and, 10

Beyond the Asterisk
Understanding Native Students in Higher Education
Edited by Heather J. Shotton, Shelly C. Lowe, and Stephanie J. Waterman
Foreword by John L. Garland

"Within this important and long overdue addition to the literature, higher education faculty, and administrators, have important new resources for helping shift the landscape of Native American college student experiences toward success. The importance of this particular new text cannot be understated. It has been conceived, written, and edited by Native American higher education leaders and those who have made Native students a priority in their practice. My hope is that this book becomes a catalyst for new higher education practices that lead to direct, and increased support for, Native Americans and others who are vigorously working to remove the Native American asterisk from research and practice. This text also signals a renewed call-to-action for increasing the representation of Native students, faculty, and staff on our campuses."

—*John L. Garland*

Sty/us

22883 Quicksilver Drive
Sterling, VA 20166-2102

Subscribe to our e-mail alerts: www.Styluspub.com

Also available from Stylus

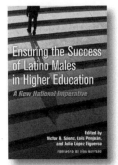

Ensuring the Success of Latino Males in Higher Education
A New National Imperative
Edited by Victor B. Sáenz, Luis Ponjuán, and Julie López Figueroa
Foreword by Aída Hurtado

The contributors to this book present new research on factors that inhibit or promote Latino success in both four-year institutions and community colleges in order to inform both policy and practice. They explore the social-cultural factors, peer dynamics, and labor force demands that may be perpetuating the growing gender gap, and consider what lessons can be learned from research on the success of Latinas. This book also closely examines key practices that enable first generation Latino male undergraduates to succeed which may seem counterintuitive to institutional expectations and preconceived notions of student behavior.

While uncovering the lack of awareness at all levels of our colleges and universities about the depth and severity of the challenges facing Latino males, this book provides the foundation for rethinking policy; challenges leaders to institutionalize male-focused programs and services; and presents data to inform needed changes in practice for outreach and retention.

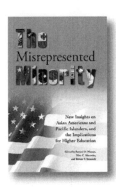

The Misrepresented Minority
New Insights on Asian Americans and Pacific Islanders, and the Implications for Higher Education
Edited by Samuel D. Museus, Dina C. Maramba, and Robert T. Teranishi

"Covering topics from identity to activism and admissions to the glass ceiling, this ground-breaking volume fills a gaping hole in higher educational research on Asian Americans and Pacific Islanders. Using critical theories, national data sets, and case studies, scholars provide campuses with new findings and approaches to address the unequal treatment of AAPI students and faculty."

—Shirley Hune,
Professor of Educational Leadership and Policy Studies, University of Washington

"This book assembles an extensive array of extraordinarily authentic accounts of Asian American and Pacific Islander experiences. Each chapter uniquely synthesizes theory, research, and practice to inform efforts to effectuate positive campus environments for AAPIs. A must-read for policymakers, educators, and students who seek new insights and approaches to help AAPI college students succeed."

—Doris Ching,
Emeritus Vice President for Student Affairs, University of Hawaii System